361.7
KEL

30.00

Sutton County Library
306 E. Mulberry St.
Sonora, TX 76950
325-387-2111

DATE DUE

THE FOUNDATIONS OF

TEXAN
PHILANTHROPY

NUMBER NINETY-EIGHT:
Centennial Series of the Association of
Former Students, Texas A&M University

THE FOUNDATIONS OF

TEXAN PHILANTHROPY

Mary L. Kelley

Texas A&M University Press
College Station

Library of Congress Cataloging-in-Publication Data
Kelley, Mary L., 1949–
    The foundations of Texan philanthropy / Mary L. Kelley .— 1st ed.
        p. cm. — (Centennial series of the Association of Former Students, Texas A&M
    University ; no. 98)
    Includes bibliographical references and index.
    ISBN 1-58544-327-1 (cloth : alk. paper)
    1. Philanthropists—Texas—Biography.   2. Millionaires—Texas—Biography.
3. Charitable uses, trusts, and foundations—Texas—History.   4. Humanitarianism—
Texas—History.   5. Social action—Texas—History.   6. Corporations—Charitable
contributions—Texas—History.   I. Title.   II. Series.
HV98.T5K45 2004
361.7′4′0922764—dc22
                                                                            2003018574

♾ The paper used in this book meets the minimum requirements of the American National Standard
for Permanence of Paper for Printed Library Materials, Z39.48-1984.
Binding materials have been chosen for durability.

For my parents, Jim and Margaret Searls

CONTENTS

ILLUSTRATIONS

PREFACE

Historians and writers alike have frequently depicted the story of Texas as a progression of heroic conquests over a raw land and its native inhabitants. Nineteenth-century images of pioneer families subduing a parched landscape, dust-covered cowboys corralling Longhorn herds, U.S. cavalrymen waging ethnic wars against Native Americans, and fearless Texas Rangers enforcing frontier justice have dominated the literature—at times assuming almost mythical proportions. Lawlessness and violence have also coursed through these much-celebrated narratives. Then, after the turn of the century, accounts of oilmen or "wildcatters" embellished this enduring legacy, perpetuating traits of rugged individualism, fierce competitiveness, and spirited independence. Popular culture as well, through music, motion pictures, and television, romanticized and then immortalized these colorful stereotypes. This narrow concentration on the pre-industrial frontier experience fostered a one-dimensional depiction of Texas—one that denied the complexity and diversity of the state.

As scholars now acknowledge, another side of the Texas character existed. In addition to such larger-than-life heroes and legends, whose rousing stories have been well-documented, the Lone Star State also produced concerned citizens who promoted philanthropic endeavors. Beginning in 1920 and continuing to the present day, Texans have established more than three thousand private foundations for charitable, educational, scientific, and cultural purposes. Their largess and generosity helped define the Texas experience as much as their combativeness and grit. As such, they became a major force for social, educational, and cultural change in Texas, thereby providing a more inclusive picture of the state.

Yet, except on a national scale, few scholars have explored the topic at the state or local levels. Biographies of well-known philanthropists such as Andrew Carnegie and John D. Rockefeller Sr. are abundant, and histories of their bequests to public libraries, symphony halls, and major universities are familiar. Recent works on their large-scale foundations are also plentiful. Little scholarship, however, has occurred concerning Texas donors and their benefactions. In *The New Handbook of Texas* (1996), an essential reference tool for Texas history, no entry exists for philanthropy, nor do any secondary sources occur for various foundations. The founders, their gifts, their institutions, and their visions for their communities remain largely unexamined.

The absence of a systematic study of organized philanthropy in Texas has been an oversight, yet an understandable omission. Foundations comprise only a small fraction, 7 to 9 percent, of all charitable giving and, heretofore, have received more attention from sociologists and economists than from historians. Moreover, the private papers of philanthropic organizations, with the exception of income tax returns and annual reports, are not always part of the public record, thereby discouraging scholarship. Donors and grant makers also have shunned scrutiny, preferring instead anonymity. For example, some have believed that charitable giving was meritorious only if accomplished without personal aggrandizement or self-promotion. Others have carefully guarded their privacy, arguing for their right to allocate personal funds in confidence. And still others have feared that needless publicity would bring unsolicited "begging letters" or hostile congressional investigations. As a consequence, facts and statistics are not always easy to assemble.

Even with unlimited access to substantial files, recording foundation histories is difficult. Often official records such as board minutes and annual reports, written for public consumption, do not reveal the spirit, vision, and motivation of founders, board, and staff. Many questions remain for the historian, who must tease out the answers. For example: Who determines the grant-making process? Who controls its assets? Is the foundation philosophically or ideologically driven? What grant proposals were rejected and why? How has the foundation changed over time? What relationships exist with other foundations?

Scholarly research on early Texas foundations posed similar challenges. As an outsider seeking access to private archives, I experienced a wide range of receptions, from enthusiastic cooperation to guarded acceptance to outright refusal. Of those organizations researched, several provided comfortable environments in which to work—ample refreshments, copying services, and even free books and materials. Others offered only cursory visits with restricted access to important files. And a few showed scant interest, preferring authorized foundation histories and admiring founder biographies instead. Not surprisingly, these in-house publications offered portraits without warts and narratives without historical context. All, however, granted oral interviews either with the foundation director, staff officer, or family member.

Despite these barriers to research, or because of them, I imposed certain limitations on this study. Due to the large number of foundations in existence, I decided to focus on the origins and legacies of a few pioneering institutions. Specifically, I selected the George Brackenridge Foundation due to its pathbreaking position as the first organized in the state. Similarly, The Dallas Foundation represented the earliest community foundation, while the Houston Endowment was one of the richest. The Hogg Foundation for Mental Health, the first established by a Texas woman, epitomized the professionalization in foundation management. Furthermore, the Amon Carter Foundation embodied another important development—the role of organized philanthropy in the support of the arts. And the Conference of Southwest Foundations organized the first community of foundations in the nation. All were established between 1920 and 1950 and provided a representative sample—from different major cities, geographical regions, and time periods in Texas. Then, I extended their development to 1970, the year after the passage of the Tax Reform Act of 1969. This law, a turning point in organized philanthropy, served as a natural stopping place for my research.

The omission of many early foundations from this study, however, does not in any way diminish their equally important role to the development of organized philanthropy in Texas. For example, the Moody Foundation (1942), after an initial period of inactivity, has made a huge difference in the quality of life both in Galveston County and throughout the state. The Moody Foundation's colorful history has already been reported, as has that of the Galveston Kempner Fund (1946) and several others. Likewise, the Meadows Foundation (1948), a model family trust, has provided innovation and leadership in the world of philanthropy, receiving numerous awards for its creativity. These Texas foundations and countless others have significantly altered the social and cultural landscape of the state. As such their history and contributions deserve to be told and offer possibilities for future research and scholarship. (A complete listing of early Texas foundations can be found in Table 1 of the Appendix.)

The history of early Texas foundations has also necessarily been restricted to an account from "the top down." As Ford Foundation staff member and scholar Waldemar A. Nielson has pointed out in *Inside American Philanthropy*, grant-making institutions begin with a person—usually a wealthy donor—not with an overarching vision or strategic plan. The role of ordinary citizens, many of whom were humble supplicants or grant recipients, therefore, has not been within the scope of this study; such a "bottom-up" analysis, however, warrants attention by future scholars. As a consequence, chapters one through five not only chronicle the genesis of foundation philanthropy in Texas, but also pose several biographical questions: Who were the early founders? What were their motivations? What were the sources of their gifts? How did they use their wealth to leverage social or cultural change? What were their legal constraints and economic incentives? What were their lasting legacies? Chapter six on the Conference of Southwest Foundations recounts the developing philanthropic community in Texas and includes new sources previously unavailable to scholars.

Given the fact that foundations are not the dominant source for charitable support, surpassed in individual giving by approximately 85 percent, why the disproportionate interest? First, the overall scale of their assets is considerable. Such vast accumulation of discretionary funds in elite institutions has always tended to fascinate the average person and arouse the attention of watchdog groups. Second, donors to philanthropic organizations are usually highly successful, visible men and women who command wealth and power. As such, they naturally attract loyal allies and staunch enemies, who, in turn, draw public scrutiny. Third, interest in institutional philanthropy exceeds its numbers precisely because it is organized and, hence, somewhat more readily observed. Fourth, foundations hold a unique position in the

American polity, serving both private and public purposes. As independent funding agents, they provide important services to the community, while preserving individual initiative and freedom of expression.

But, at the same time, the autonomous and undemocratic nature of tax-exempt private foundations has fostered suspicions concerning the unregulated concentration of wealth. With government budgetary cuts, grant makers occasionally functioned as de facto policy makers, thereby shaping vital decisions over the allocation of scarce resources. Accordingly, private foundations in a democratic society must therefore maintain their institutional legitimacy by conforming to a degree of control. Beginning in 1955 the Ford Foundation and a few others led the way in recognizing this distinctive public-private role by becoming less secretive and opening their archives.

Scholarly research on the role of philanthropy and foundations in American society, however, was sluggish. Many private foundations continued to discourage inquiries into their operations, hoping to avoid outside scrutiny, particularly from congressional investigations. But gradually, as philanthropic work became more professionalized, foundation officers began to recognize the value of scholarly research and its potential for self-examination, public accountability, and institutional improvement. In turn, they became more transparent. Many began to place their records in local archives and even to provide research grants to scholars. Only within the last few decades has access to foundation files significantly increased, thereby attracting historians and others across the social disciplines. While this trend has provided opportunities for more open exchanges between scholars and practitioners, much still remains to be done. This volume represents the first attempt to document the important role of early Texas foundations to channel their tax-free, private wealth for the public good.

ACKNOWLEDGMENTS

From conception to completion of this manuscript, I have incurred significant debts. Several individuals and institutions have made this book possible and the dissertation that preceded it. Officers and staff at numerous philanthropic foundations were particularly helpful, especially Gilbert M. Denman Jr. of the Brackenridge Foundation, Mary Jalonick with The Dallas Foundation, Steven Fenberg of the Houston Endowment, Ralph E. Culler III with the Hogg Foundation for Mental Health, Ruth Carter Stevenson and John Robinson of the Amon G. Carter Foundation, and Maud Keeling and Lucille de Dominico with the Conference of Southwest Foundations. Attorney Gina De Gennaro of San Antonio proofed the manuscript for legal accuracy while the Center for American History in Austin supported my research with a generous travel grant.

I am also indebted to several scholars. Early in my career Dr. Steven Boyd at the University of Texas at San Antonio consistently showed confidence in my abilities and graciously extended library privileges throughout my research. Dr. Ron Tyler, director of the Texas State Historical Association, suggested the topic, while Dr. Howell Smith of Wake Forest University critiqued some of the early chapters and provided invaluable insight into the topic.

Members of the Texas Christian University faculty aided me immeasurably as well. Dr. Mark T. Gilderhus and Dr. Sara Sohmer reviewed this manuscript, offering useful suggestions and valuable comments for its improvement. Dr. Ben Procter, a.k.a. "Simon," merits special recognition. I am especially grateful for his unflagging enthusiasm, scholarly guidance, and steady encouragement. He meticulously reviewed my manuscript, offered constructive criticism, and thereby made me a better writer and historian.

But, most of all, I am indebted to my late parents who instilled in me the desire to learn and the will to never give up. To them, I dedicate this book.

INTRODUCTION
Habits of the Heart

F OUNDATION PHILANTHROPY, or organized private giving for the public good, was largely a product of the early twentieth century. Beginning in 1907 with the creation of the first modern, general-purpose foundation, the Russell Sage Foundation, Gilded Age millionaires such as steel master Andrew Carnegie, oil baron John D. Rockefeller Sr., and heiress Margaret Olivia Sage sought socially acceptable methods to dispose of their surplus income. Overwhelmed by the magnitude of their fortunes, made possible by laissez-faire economics, as well as influenced by the Progressive era "search for order" through efficiency and organization, these nouveau riche yearned for a more systematic approach to the allocation of their charitable dollars. They also held a buoyantly optimistic faith that major social problems such as poverty and illness could be solved. Rather than the temporary palliative aid of individual beneficence or spontaneous almsgiving, a few affluent donors advocated a basic attack on deeper long-term causes through the application of "scientific philanthropy." For example, they believed that a cure for a disease was a better goal than another hospital for the sick. And they prized research to improve crop yields more than supporting soup kitchens.[1]

As prosperous beneficiaries of American capitalism, potential philanthropists looked to the business world with its professional management and corporate governance to model a new institution for their largess. Rockefeller, founder of the Standard Oil Company of New Jersey, convincingly argued in 1909: "If a combination to do business is effective in saving waste and in getting better results, why is not a combination far more important in philanthropic work?" Accordingly, after the turn of the century, "wholesale philanthropy" through the modern foundation gained favor with many of the charitably inclined elite. Rather than the more traditional "retail" style of individual giving, grant-making foundations separated the donor from the recipient and offered a sound, rational alternative for the distribution of private wealth for the public good.[2]

Several characteristics distinguished this new form of organized benevolence. In general, early foundations shared certain common traits: a generous donor; a principal sum with investment income; a broad, general purpose; a duration of a specified number of years or in perpetuity; a nonprofit, tax-exempt status; a geographical focus; and a board of trustees with a professional staff. Taking their cue from the corporate world, grant makers also infused their language with business metaphors: founding charters, trust agreements, legal incorporation, managed funds, mission statements, boards of trustees, and grant assessments. As private foundations achieved a critical mass of approximately 5,000 nationwide by mid-century, they comprised a unique and significant part of America's growing nonprofit third sector—affecting public policy, effecting social change, and spurring congressional reaction.[3]

Yet like all social inventions, philanthropic foundations and the altruistic ideals that they represented had roots in an earlier era. The first American philanthropists were most likely the native inhabitants of San Salvador and Hispaniola who, in 1492, Christopher Columbus observed, were "ingenuous and free" with their possessions to his men after landfall in the New World. In 1621 the initial Thanksgiving commemorated early acts of voluntary giving by the Native Americans who had helped the early colonists adapt to their new environment. But not until 1630 was love of mankind—the Greek definition of philanthropy—openly endorsed. Massachusetts Bay Governor John Winthrop, in his sermon "A Modell [sic] of Christian Charity" on board the *Arbella,* sternly reminded his fellow colonists of their covenant with God. Every person, he admonished, must "afford his help to another in every want and distress" in the New World. Furthermore, Winthrop encouraged those of greater means to aid "the poor and inferior sort" through the Old World practice of *noblesse oblige,* a concept that linked the duties of the wealthy to the society that had enriched them. The rich existed, therefore, to be stewards of God's wealth.[4]

In the wilderness, devoid of government structures and a hereditary aristocracy, these ideals acquired new meaning. The doctrine of civic stewardship—the notion that successful individuals owed a dual obligation of time and money to society—gained favor. Soon other Anglican appeals for benevolence appeared. *Magnalia* (1702) and *Essays to Do Good* (1710) by clergyman Cotton Mather provided further evidence of New World "philanthropic dynamism" and its important role in preserving the community and encouraging public virtue.[5]

Over a century after the first colonists built their "city upon a hill," the creation of the new American Republic with a limited government fostered individual giving through private philanthropy. Fearing the rebirth of monarchy and the growth of a large bureaucracy, the framers of the Constitution restricted the powers of the central government, delegating all others to the states or the people. The preservation of a vibrant civil society, Thomas Jefferson contended, characterized by active citizen participation, was essential to a strong democracy. Thus, by adopting a divided federal system with a Bill of Rights protecting individual liberties, the founders established the theoretical underpinnings for private philanthropy, thereby ensuring the existence of a third sector, of which foundations composed only a small part.

By the nineteenth century, Alexis de Tocqueville, a French social philosopher and visitor to the United States, argued in 1835 for the centrality of the private, voluntary sector in his classic book *Democracy in America.* "Americans of all ages, all stations in life, and all types of disposition, are forever forming associations . . . to give fetes, found seminaries, build churches, distribute books, and send missionaries to the antipodes." Citizens of the United States, he further observed, relied on each other for those needs—such as hospitals and schools—that government neglected or failed to fund. By forming associations, they addressed concerns not supported by the majority. Private initiative for the public good, thus, became an important part of the nation's social and cultural development, thereby preserving individual freedom and a degree of pluralism.[6]

Such acts of mutual helpfulness and unparalleled generosity reflected a basic trait in the American character. Tocqueville, who was a keen observer of "manners and mores," had discerned these unselfish attributes, or "habits of the heart," while on his nine-month tour of the nation, 1831–32. Not only did Americans form "associations of a thousand other kinds" for a myriad of purposes, he observed, but they also "spontaneously and eagerly" lent assistance to one another whenever needed. If some unexpected disaster did strike, he continued, "a thousand strangers willingly open their purses, and small but very numerous gifts relieve their distress." British author James Bryce, more than a half century later (1888), also noted this charitable cultural pattern. "Nowhere," he observed, "is money so readily given for any public purpose" or "so many acts of private kindness done" than in the United States.[7]

Scholars also supported their judgment. In 1953 Harvard University historian Arthur M. Schlesinger Sr. persuasively asserted that "unlike Europe, the United States has fathered few misers." Successful citizens, he contended, have always "shared their money with others almost as freely as they made it, returning at least part of their substance to channels of social usefulness through munificent gifts and bequests." And in 1957 Professor Merle Curti of the University of Wisconsin convincingly argued that "philanthropy has been one of the major aspects of and keys to American social and cultural development," indeed—one of its deepest core values.[8]

Charity and philanthropy, although closely related and frequently used interchangeably, were nevertheless distinct concepts. The first precept arose from the Judeo-Christian tradition. As Saint Paul wrote in his first letter to the Corinthians: "And now abideth faith, hope, and charity, these three; but the greatest of these is charity." With a scriptural mandate, religious leaders therefore admonished their congregations to perform charitable works directed at the poor and needy. This concern for the welfare of others was necessarily personal and compassionate. For instance, good Samaritans generously donated to widows and orphans and voluntarily assisted travelers in need. Devout Christians routinely tithed ten percent of their income as "a religiously sanctioned gift to God and the poor." Acts of charity, therefore, were outward signs of religious faith, as well as a hope of salvation.[9]

Philanthropy, however, according to Professor Robert H. Bremner of Ohio State University, covered a much wider field, specifically the "improvement in the quality of human life." As a broadly defined secular term, it was more impersonal and dispassionate but, equally important, more acceptable to modern civic stewards such as Carnegie and Rockefeller who sought long-term solutions rather than temporary aid. For instance, Carnegie insisted in his classic 1889 treatise "Wealth," that bestowing charity on the "unreclaimably poor" caused more injury by encouraging "the very evils which it proposes to mitigate or cure." Rockefeller claimed in 1909 that "the help that does the most good and the least harm" was not "what is usually called charity." Only "the investment of effort or money, carefully considered," he asserted, comprised the best form of philanthropy. As a consequence, enlightened giving that was both planned and meaningful, especially through grant-making foundations, represented a break from Victorian era charity. Thus, by aiding the "fit," Carnegie sanctimoniously proclaimed, and by providing "ladders upon which the aspiring can rise," such as libraries and schools, the condition of mankind would improve.[10]

With a paradigm shift away from individual benevolence and toward organized giving in the first decade of the twentieth century, a "philanthropic revolution" occurred, and a fundamentally different vehicle—the general-purpose, professionally managed foundation—emerged. But no one model prevailed. In fact, several types—independent, operating, corporate, and community—resulted; however, divisions between categories were often ambiguous, and lines frequently blurred. Moreover, some organizations utilized the term "foundation" without meeting the strict definition of a nonprofit, grant-making institution that administered private wealth for the public good. Adding further confusion was a diverse nomenclature for the same entity: foundation, corporation, institute, endowment, trust, fund, benefit, institution, account, society, company, memorial, and commission.[11]

Nevertheless, the vehicle used by all parties for establishing a philanthropic foundation was the same—a trust instrument executed by a principal donor or family. The agreement was either testamentary, consisting of a will establishing a trust to serve as the vehicle for the foundation, or a deed of gift effective during a lifetime. A written charter also commonly delineated the benefactor's purpose either in broad language, thereby giving the trustees wide discretion, or in precise terms, restricting funds to a particular field of human need. Length of tenure, usually for fifty years or in perpetuity, and geographical focus—local, state, national, or international—were also adumbrated. In the case of larger foundations, an application for incorporation under state laws completed their legal status, thereby providing easier access to tax-exempt status and limiting trustee liability.[12]

Four distinct classifications of foundations emerged, depending on the initial endowment, mission statement, and funding source. The independent foundation was the most common, usually the product of a single donor or family for some charitable purpose. Using 1960 statistics, the earliest date for reliable data, 5,202 foundations existed in the United States, with 3,184, or 62 percent, comprising this first category. Somewhat different were the corporate, or company-sponsored, foundations. They received their funds from profit-making businesses that were legally distinct from contribution programs administered by the corporation. Altogether, 1,333 operated in the United States, or approximately 25 percent. Community foundations formed a third category. Organized much like a family foundation, they derived their resources from several donors, with a citizen board allocating funds for local needs. Nationwide, 101 existed, representing 2 percent. Although most private foundations specialized in grant making, the primary purpose of the fourth category—operating foundations—was to direct specified research or social programs, usually as a part of their own initiatives. They accounted for 584, or about 11 percent of all foundations in the United States.[13]

Four stages of foundation activity occurred in the early evolution of organized philanthropy. In the initial proto-development period, 1880–1910, as the United States became the foremost industrial power in the world, surpassing even England and Germany, a few lucky and talented entrepreneurs acquired colossal wealth at a rate previously unimaginable. The number of millionaires—a term originally coined by British statesman Benjamin Disraeli in 1826, but only popularly used during the 1890s—dramatically surged from fewer than 100 individuals in 1880 to almost 40,000 by 1910. Furthermore, at the turn of the century approximately 8 percent of American families reportedly controlled more than 75 percent of the nation's real property. Unencumbered by federal regulations or tax laws, their income, according to Baptist clergyman and Rockefeller advisor Frederick T. Gates, "roll[ed] up like an avalanche," reaching immense proportions. For example, Carnegie, at the time he sold his steel interests in 1901, held assets valued at more than $350 million. Russell Sage, upon his death in 1906, was worth over $65 million, acquired from lumber, railroads, and banking. And Rockefeller, even with the dissolution of Standard Oil of New Jersey in 1910, became the nation's first billionaire.[14]

But generosity and altruism were as characteristic of the era as acquisitiveness and self-interest. The amassing of huge capital by controlling key industries incurred enormous responsibilities for its charitable distribution. In fact, Carnegie wrote that the major problem of his age was "the proper administration of wealth." Without a swift, planned schedule of giving, escalating riches of these millionaires, Gates warned with evangelical fervor, would eventually "crush you and your children and your children's children!" As a consequence, a few owners of Gilded Age fortunes (approximately 2 percent) began to rethink the proper use and disposition of their excess funds. Their reexamination resulted in Carnegie's writing "Wealth" in 1889; Rockefeller's hiring Gates two years later as his full-time philanthropic adviser; and Margaret Olivia Sage's penning in 1905 "The Opportunities and Responsibilities of Leisured Women." All ultimately concluded that a philanthropic foundation, organized around broad principles and managed by a staff of experts, best exemplified the proper distribution of private wealth for the public good.[15]

During the next period, 1910–30, foundation philanthropy waxed and then waned. Several large, general-purpose foundations emerged, including the Carnegie Corporation of New York (1911), the Rockefeller Foundation (1913), the Rosenwald Fund (1917), and the Duke Endowment (1924). As the nation urbanized, such community foundations as the Cleveland Foundation (1914) organized with a more localized focus. "Black Tuesday," October 29, 1929, however, abruptly ended the optimism of the era. With the stock market crash and a subsequent decade-long depression, a gradual erosion of foundation assets occurred. The enthusiasm for broad, long-term philanthropic pursuits ebbed in the face of more immediate, massive suffering.[16]

From 1930 to 1945 foundation activities, in competition with New Deal programs, initially abated but gradually revived, forging a public-private partnership. The unprecedented economic crisis had destroyed public confidence in private philanthropy, thereby shifting individual loyalties to government solutions. As a result, the growing welfare state with its overlapping alphabet agencies supplanted many nongovernment-funded projects, causing many Americans to wonder if private philanthropy would survive. But philanthropic organizations rebounded with the passage of higher income tax rates in 1935, as well as with the added incentive of corporate charitable deductions (up to 5 percent of taxable income). Moreover, President Franklin D. Roosevelt's increasingly strident antibusiness rhetoric after 1936 sparked renewed interest in organized giving, especially among potential corporate donors, as an important counterweight to the growth of federal power. By 1941, however, wartime conditions and the perceived threat to American interests from fascism and communism served to promote closer ties between the public and private sectors. As a consequence, the federal government and philanthropic foundations formed a crucial partnership to help organize the war effort, deliver necessary services, and plan the postwar world order.[17]

Paradoxically, the large incursion by government into the private sector did not immediately lead to a decrease in new foundations during its fourth stage (1945–70). Rather, the period unleashed a dramatic expansion and then a gradual decline in new foundations. Fueled by the postwar prosperity, more favorable tax laws, and a lack of government regulatory restraints, the number of new grant-making organizations multiplied—one of the striking developments in private philanthropy. The 1948 directory *American Foundations and Their Fields,* initiated by the Twentieth Century Fund and continued by Raymond Rich Associates, listed 899 foundations; twenty-three years later, *The Foundation Directory* (1971) reported that 5,454 existed. Despite the fact that both sources utilized differing criteria, conservative estimates placed the increase at almost 500 percent. This upsurge in foundation philanthropy meant that the federal government increasingly relied on private funding sources to support underfunded programs, conduct new research, and direct experimental pilot programs. But during the early cold war years, the growing power of the third sector, especially autonomous grant-making organizations, also led to public outcry and legislative inquiries. No longer were their philanthropic decisions with tax-exempt money unquestionably accepted. Consequently, after 1950, as foundations became an integral part of the American polity, a sustained attack challenged their administration of private wealth for the public good. The erosion of public confidence in private philanthropy eventually led to a gradual decline in foundation births during the 1960s. The end result was the passage of the Tax Reform Act of 1969—the first major piece of legislation regulating foundation activities and their gifts.[18]

Texans also participated in full measure in the American philanthropic tradition, stemming from their frontier heritage. Despite their much-celebrated reputation as self-reliant, rugged individualists, they also volunteered their private resources for the public good. The problems involved in settling a raw, hostile land not only promoted "habits of the heart," through neighborly cooperation in time of need but also required friendly assistance to confront unexpected dangers. For example, as pioneering settlers emigrating from east of the Sabine River, they banded together to subdue troublesome Indians who threatened their communities and risked their lives in epidemic outbreaks, such as yellow fever, to tend to the sick and dying. In addition, they "constantly formed associations," including mutual aid societies to assist families and disabled Civil War veterans, women's clubs for civic purposes, and disaster-relief organizations such as the Howard Association, the first charitable organization in the Republic of Texas.[19]

But Texans also subscribed to the notion of civic stewardship, contributing both time and money to favored causes. From their growing profits in land, livestock, and crude oil, wealthy citizens used their vast fortunes to build communities and ameliorate social ills through "retail philanthropy." For example, civic-minded businessmen regularly donated their personal funds to needy projects, as well as voluntarily raised money to assist disaster victims. Wives of prominent men across the state freely contributed to the support of orphanages and women's shelters. After the turn of the century, however, and the advent of "scientific philanthropy," they also envisioned a broader, more permanent vehicle to address better their diverse problems. In every region of the state, from the Piney Woods and Gulf Coast to the West Texas high plains and Rio Grande valley, wealthy donors converted to "wholesale giving" by creating philanthropic organizations, primarily to benefit the citizens of Texas. (See Table 4.) As sociologist Robert Sutherland, "the most knowledgeable person in the Southwest on matters relative to philanthropic foundations," tersely observed: "People [Texans] like to make money and they also like to give money."[20]

Private foundations in Texas lagged behind northern and eastern states—but not for long. In 1930, the majority of all sizable grant-making organizations emerged in regions with large concentrations of wealth, namely, New York with 48 percent nationwide, and the five industrialized states of Pennsylvania, Massachusetts, Ohio, Michigan, and Illinois with 29 percent overall. By 1960, however, New York totaled only 26 percent, and the other northeastern states comprised 30 percent. The Southwest recorded one of the biggest gains. Although some of the apparent growth was due to increased reportage, Texas registered the largest number in the region with 217 new foundations, or approximately 4 percent of the total.[21]

Organized philanthropy emerged in Texas during the second stage (1910–30) of national development. Its "founding moment" was the creation of the George W. Brackenridge Foundation (1920) in San Antonio through a bequest in his will. As the first modern Texas philanthropist, publisher-banker Brackenridge had benefited financially from Gilded Age economics. Although his fortune did not approach the fabled wealth of Carnegie or Rockefeller, he too was concerned about his mounting funds. Influenced by the doctrines of civic stewardship and Social Darwinism—a concept that applied evolutionary theory to the unequal distribution of wealth—Brackenridge therefore devoted much of his time and income to benefit the people of Texas. In turn, his pioneering efforts served as a model to other wealthy Texans to establish philanthropic institutions. Consequently, by 1928 eight new private foundations resulted from large family fortunes. (See Tables 1 and 2.) Then, in 1929 the first community trust—The Dallas Foundation—emerged in Texas, only fifteen years after Judge Frederick H. Goff of Cleveland set the pattern. By the end of the decade, Texas boasted a total of nine philanthropic foundations.[22]

The next stage of foundation development (1930–45) in Texas also mirrored national trends. In the early years of the Great Depression (1930–35), the creation of new foundations was sluggish. Texans founded only eleven such institutions. But after the mid-1930s, with increases in the federal tax codes, many upper-income Texans turned to large-scale, organized giving to reduce their financial obligations. World War II spurred additional grant-making organizations, as donors once again faced extremely high income and estate taxes. Thus, by the beginning of 1945, wealthy Texans had created fifty-three more new foundations, including the Houston Endowment (1937), one of the largest in the state, and the Hogg Foundation for Mental Health (1940), the first professionally managed, philanthropic institution associated with the University of Texas—and founded by a Texas woman.[23]

From 1945 to 1970 Texas foundations came of age, experiencing both tremendous growth and unprecedented public scrutiny. During the early postwar years, considered by many experts as an "Age of Foundations," their numbers swelled from approximately 73 to 247, an increase of 238 percent! Two important developments were the creation of the Amon G. Carter Foundation (1945) for large-scale "cultural philanthropy" and the organization of the Conference of Southwest Foundations (1948), the first regional philanthropic community in the nation. In the volatile cold war atmosphere, not everyone viewed private philanthropy positively, though. Congressional investigations targeted several Texas foundations—including the Houston Endowment, the Carter Foundation, and seven others. As a result of some long-standing abuses and a few glaring cases of misconduct, the new Tax Reform Act of 1969 placed private grant-making institutions in Texas, as well as in the rest of the nation, under strict federal oversight. Yet despite the previous negative publicity, which resulted in the nadir of organized philanthropy, by 1970 Texas ranked sixth nationwide in the number of private foundations.[24]

From 1920 to 1970 economic and demographic factors contributed to the overall growth in Texas foundations. In particular, the rise of the oil and natural gas industry after the 1901 discovery at Spindletop, with its profitable federal tax breaks, produced a second Gilded Age, thereby providing much of the necessary seed money for wealthy Texans to endow philanthropic institutions. At the same time, the local economy diversified to include not only oil refining, but also meat packing, flour milling, lumbering, publishing, cottonseed, and construction. The rapid population increase in Texas, a Sunbelt state, from 6.4 million in 1940 to 9.5 million by 1960, and the rapid growth of its major cities were also factors. As the state followed national trends and urbanized, attendant health, education, and social problems soon followed. The allocation of scarce resources rapidly began to outstrip the demands of a changing society.

To meet the needs of a less isolated, less rural, and more diverse population, private Texas foundations, most located in mid-to-large-size cities, increasingly stepped in to channel financial support to educational, religious, charitable, and cultural endeavors. (See Table 5.) As Sutherland observed, organized private giving was "based on the philosophy that government does not have to do everything." Texans, inherently wary of a distant administration to solve their problems, seemingly agreed. So as more and more individuals amassed huge fortunes, as tax codes provided incentives to practice private philanthropy, and as federal and state governments failed to serve human needs, from 1920 to 1970 Texans established approximately 250 private foundations across the state, thereby leveraging their private wealth for the public good.[25]

ONE

THE GOSPEL OF WEALTH ACCORDING TO ST. GEORGE

George W. Brackenridge and the Beginning of
Organized Philanthropy in Texas, 1920

O N DECEMBER 28, 1920, GEORGE W. BRACKENRIDGE, San Antonio banker, newspaper publisher, and real estate developer, died peacefully at his home, Fernridge, leaving an estate with an estimated worth of approximately $3 million. In the extant will, originally written on September 8, 1913, Brackenridge bequeathed all his property to his legal heirs and, more importantly, to the citizens of Texas. He then appointed the San Antonio Loan and Trust Company to administer all of his "real, personal and mixed" assets and allocate lifetime incomes to designated family members, loyal servants, and valued friends, as well as selected charities. He further stipulated that the remainder of his wealth, after payment of debts, would be used "for educational purposes"—a reflection of his philanthropic spirit. Moreover, he specified that these excess funds would strictly aid students in attending their institutions, not for infrastructure such as buildings or classrooms. Although numerous hand-written codicils spanning a five-year period amended his personal dispersals, Brackenridge never significantly altered the original intent or terms of his will.[1]

In the aftermath of Brackenridge's death, a four-year legal battle ensued—a common occurrence with sizable estates. Two nieces, Isabella McIntyre and Isabella Roberts, contested the will, claiming that he had written a second one just prior to his parting. During the court proceedings, several witnesses asserted that they saw Brackenridge execute a new document and affix his signature. Others, such as University of Texas President Robert E. Vinson, testified that Brackenridge intended to write another testament that would specify land and funds to expand the Austin campus. As a longtime advocate of the university and a member of its board of regents, Brackenridge, sometimes referred to as its "patron saint," had repeatedly expressed his desire to relocate the school to a larger, more attractive tract near the Colorado River; but he left no specific bequest to the university to do so. The trustees of the estate, however, remained resolute, steadfastly refusing to concede the existence of an additional will. As a consequence, the legal case dragged on.[2]

The resolution of the court dispute hinged on the validity of the 1913 document. According to the law, if a new instrument had been written, the previous one would become "null and void." When a second will never materialized, and two separate judges questioned the legality of the first instrument, the court ruled that Brackenridge had died intestate—that is, without a will. Biographer Marilyn

McAdams Sibley speculated that either "Brackenridge destroyed it, someone else did, or it was in some manner lost forever." Whatever its fate, by revoking the original testament, the legal system sanctioned the division of his property among his rightful heirs—another potentially thorny problem.[3]

By 1925, the inheritors, trustees, and plaintiffs, tiring of the financial and legal impasse, settled out of court and permitted the original will to be probated. But the final outcome proved unsatisfactory to all parties—save one. The plaintiffs, McIntyre and Roberts, failed to secure the additional funds allotted in the 1913 will and altered by subsequent codicils. The University of Texas, expecting a monetary windfall, received only the income from a small grant, not the entire Brackenridge fortune as erroneously reported by a local newspaper. And Eleanor Brackenridge, sister and guardian of his legal papers,

George W. Brackenridge. From the *San Antonio Light* Collection, no. 3334-F, courtesy U.T. Institute of Texan Cultures at San Antonio.

died in 1924 before the lawsuit was ever finalized. The clear victors in the contest, therefore, were Texas students. As an advocate of "the intellectual equalization of man," Brackenridge had posthumously provided for an educational fund to aid "deserving young citizens of the United States." And the legal instrument he employed to accomplish this philanthropic purpose was a permanent trust fund—the George W. Brackenridge Foundation, the first of its kind in Texas.[4]

Through his public and private giving, Brackenridge pioneered organized philanthropy in the state. Like many benefactors of his age, he had supported numerous worthy causes during his life, but none more assiduously than the University of Texas. His many grants included funds to construct Brackenridge Hall in Austin, which was a dormitory for men, as well as land for a recreational park in San Antonio and money for a new public high school that bore his name. In later years, however, Brackenridge became convinced that his most enduring legacy would be to "the education of poor boys and girls equally as may be without reference to the school or college they attend." Such an endeavor, he acknowledged on his eightieth birthday, would "continue to grow and spread and do far-reaching good" long after his death. He therefore purposefully left the bulk of his estate to a more permanent institution, a foundation, to carry forward his wishes. Although his trust fund did not become a reality until after his demise in 1920, he was, according to Sibley, "one of the pioneers in the establishment of philanthropic foundations"—only eight years after the Pennsylvania steelmaker-turned-philanthropist Andrew Carnegie set the pattern.[5]

The life and career of George Brackenridge paralleled that of Carnegie, who at age fifty-four had authored "Wealth" (1889)—the classic essay on American philanthropy. Born on January 14, 1832, three years prior to Carnegie, Brackenridge resided first in Indiana before settling in Jackson County, Texas. Like Carnegie, he was the scion of a Presbyterian family, growing up in modest surroundings with family roots in Scotland. A Union sympathizer, he avoided military service during the Civil War—as did Carnegie—and reaped financial success through opportunistic business practices, building a cotton empire in South Texas. As a Republican in a Democratic state, he also served as United States Treasury agent before moving in 1866 to San Antonio, a city of approximately 10,000 residents. Believing that "profit is one of the essential things," he further enlarged his fortune as president of the San Antonio National Bank, owner of the San Antonio Water Works Company, director of the Express Publishing Company, founder of the San Antonio Loan and Trust, and holder of numerous land parcels throughout the state. As a result, Brackenridge, a self-made "man of wealth" by age fifty, joined Carnegie and a growing number of nouveau riche as Gilded Age millionaires by the fin de siècle.[6]

Brackenridge also possessed an uncanny resemblance to the Pennsylvania ironmaker, as well as a similar philosophy. Standing six feet tall, with piercing eyes and graying beard, the San Antonio financier—like Carnegie—dressed the part of a prosperous businessman, wearing a dark, vested suit, embellished with a watch and fob, and a felt-brimmed hat. Brackenridge also read many of the same books as Carnegie, keeping works by Charles Darwin, Thomas Huxley, and Herbert Spencer on his bedside table. A "man of thought," he constantly "quarreled with" these writings, which legitimized the actions of a brutal age by applying evolutionary doctrines of natural selection and "survival of the fittest" as scientific justification for unrestrained competition. Despite his disquietude over the unbridled concentration of wealth, he envisioned a society much as Carnegie advocated, one in which the gifted "few" would administer to the masses by creating "ladders upon which the aspiring can rise." Institutional benefactions, such as free libraries, public parks, and black schools, he contended, would return excess riches to the communities from which they had been garnered. Finally, in 1920, after experiencing much of the social and economic upheavals of the nineteenth century, yet also profiting handsomely from the emerging industrial order, Brackenridge died within months of Carnegie at the age of eighty-eight.[7]

As a contemporary of Carnegie, Brackenridge knew much about the Scottish immigrant who had amassed colossal riches while building an empire based on railroads and steel. Given his wealth, intellect, and public-spiritedness, he most likely had read "Wealth," published in the June, 1889, issue of the *North American Review.* Familiar with that scholarly journal, he had often recommended thought-provoking articles from its contents to friends. He was also fully cognizant of the Carnegie name and corporation—familiar icons to most Americans—encountering many Carnegie products in his business and civic affairs. Most importantly, Brackenridge became aware of the idea of a freestanding trust and its potential for organized, charitable giving through the Carnegie Foundation for the Advancement of Teaching (1905) and the Carnegie Corporation (1911). This new philanthropic vehicle, pioneered by Carnegie and others who had accumulated great wealth from laissez-faire economics, offered Brackenridge a rational, systematic approach to administer his surplus income; one, he observed, that would provide "the greatest good to the greatest number" and "remain and be remembered long after I have gone."[8]

As a disciple of Carnegie, Brackenridge subscribed to many of the tenets outlined in "Wealth." He believed that the accumulation of large fortunes was inevitable within a capitalist system. The inequality between rich and poor was the price society paid for competition and material comfort. Brackenridge also had little faith in the masses, endorsing Nietzsche's doctrine of the superman. "In our present state of civilization," he contended, "the few strong must take care of the weak many." They had to "strengthen themselves to carry their excessive burden" until education could ameliorate such conditions. The acquisition of great wealth, however, was not for hoarding or display but for accomplishing certain philanthropic goals. Hence, Brackenridge maintained that "men of means" were responsible for leaving the world a better place, thereby "returning their surplus wealth to the mass of their fellows in the forms best calculated to do them lasting good," as Carnegie proscribed.[9]

Brackenridge was also a model practitioner of the "Gospel of Wealth," performing many of the duties outlined by Carnegie for the monied classes. He lived a "modest, unostentatious life," shunning any display of extravagance or publicity—an important precept of Carnegie's doctrine. His original home, Fernridge, was "an unpretentious but spacious cottage," which seemed inappropriate for a man of his position. Eventually, Brackenridge constructed a second house in high Victorian style with Dutch tiles, French mirrors, and Persian rugs. "No expense or effort was spared." But he built the new home for his mother, and, upon her death in 1897, he sold the property and returned to a "simpler townhouse" adjoining the San Antonio National Bank. Although he lived well, indulging "his wants and his foibles," Brackenridge never offended the prevailing definition of good manners and unpretentious living. Neither did he care for nor seek publicity, preferring instead to live quietly and give anonymously. In fact, many of his donations remained hidden, just like his final resting place that he designed and curiously concealed behind a two-inch thick masonry wall without a gate! By intentionally keeping most of his gifts a secret, a complete record of them was never complied. Although grateful patrons later renamed some of his benefactions to reflect his generosity—changing University Hall to Brackenridge Hall and Water Works Park to Brackenridge Park—he tenaciously guarded his privacy and maintained an unobtrusive lifestyle.[10]

At the same time, Brackenridge contributed "moderately" to the legitimate needs

Brackenridge Park ca. 1920. Photo courtesy *San Antonio Express-News,* no. 69-8711, U.T. Institute of Texan Cultures at San Antonio.

of his dependents—another duty of a "man of wealth." Like Carnegie, who was married but childless, Brackenridge, a lifelong bachelor, had no descendants; hence, his estate could not pass to an offspring. He did remain devoted to his mother and sister with whom he lived. During their lifetimes Brackenridge provided for their welfare, shared his good fortune with them, and encouraged their active involvement in civic affairs. Moreover, he also contributed handsomely to loyal servants and close relatives. In later years, however, he withdrew or reduced payments to some of his beneficiaries. Believing that each generation should create its own wealth for a true meritocracy to exist, he reflected Carnegie's belief that "great sums bequeathed oftener work more for the injury than for the good of the recipients."[11]

Vast wealth, however, created one of the largest problems for Gilded Age millionaires—its "proper administration." This dilemma of surplus funds especially troubled Brackenridge. Making money was not nearly so great a task as its rightful distribution, he confided to attorney and confidant Thomas H. Franklin. "I should especially thank anyone," Brackenridge wrote, "who would show me where I could put a few hundred dollars . . . where the probability of injury is minimized." Charitable gifts and almsgiving, while well-intentioned, benefited neither the individual nor society. Thus, the pleasure of indiscriminate giving, he acerbically complained, served only to destroy individuality and self-reliance, thereby converting "good citizens into mendicants."[12]

By the mid-1880s Brackenridge realized his lifelong search for the proper distribution of excess income by adopting the solution of civic stewardship—the notion that individuals owed a dual obligation of time and money to the communities in which they lived. He therefore voluntarily served on public school and university boards. "The most important duty that a citizen has to perform," he observed, "is to protect education." Equally important, he came to regard himself as a "trustee for his poorer brethren," employing his "superior wisdom, experience, and ability" to reinvest his money where it would do the most good. Only by elevating the condition of the citizen, Brackenridge self-righteously maintained, would long-term improvement occur. Accordingly, he adapted his benevolence to encourage the "fit" to help themselves—a third duty of a "man of wealth"—rather than aid the "unworthy," which offered little "lasting good." Although Brackenridge never totally abandoned charitable "hand-outs," he increasingly applied institutional solutions, particularly "benefactions of an educational nature," to ameliorate social problems such as poverty and unemployment. As Frank G. Huntress of the *San Antonio Express* observed: "The help he extended to uncounted men and women was always the right sort of help—it encouraged them to greater effort and raised them to better things."[13]

Ironically, Brackenridge became a philanthropist at a time in American history when donors and the sources of their wealth were suspect. Muckrakers of the era, rather than upholding self-made millionaires as virtuous stewards and industrial statesmen, castigated them as robber barons, ruthless capitalists, and corporate conspirators who exploited an environment free from meddling regulations and labor restrictions. No longer were they regarded as the "most qualified" to determine the best uses for surplus income. Nor was the accumulation of vast capital unquestioned. For example, in 1895 clergyman Washington Gladden attacked Gilded Age fortunes as "tainted money," secured by "extortion or crime" and by "the most daring violation" of national laws. "Is this clean money?" he contemptuously asked. Furthermore, he chastised those charitable organizations that accepted gifts from such ill-gotten gains. For the first time, society openly began to challenge the altruistic intentions and public gifts of wealthy donors.[14]

Brackenridge also suffered rumors and allegations concerning his motives, benefactions, and business practices. Some speculated that his philanthropic intentions were tied to his unpopular Unionist activities in Texas during the Civil War. Both he and his father had profited from the war by refusing to accept Confederate money in their dry goods store in Texana. Instead, they bartered for cotton, which rose in price once the war ended, thus initiating his fortune at the expense of his neighbors. Others suspected that Brackenridge became keenly interested in education, particularly that of the black man, based on his personal resentment of the Civil War and his father's slave ownership. Supposedly, he blamed this four-year conflict for the interruption of his own long-delayed Harvard Law School training and, following emancipation, used the occasion personally to redeem the family name by aiding blacks. As a result, Brackenridge calculated the value of slave work, then resolved, as a method of partial penance, to "spend that amount of money on the race." And he did. He helped establish three elementary schools for black children in San Antonio, funded the Guadalupe Colored College in Seguin, and supported the historically black Prairie View Normal School. And still others believed that Brackenridge, frequently at odds with city leaders, hoped to redeem his reputation by supporting local education and by donating riverfront land as a San Antonio park. Whatever the reasons for his magnanimity, he never answered the charges made against him. The scathing criticism, however, added a discordant note of skepticism to his philanthropy.[15]

Like most generous men, Brackenridge's motives were mixed, ranging from altruism and humanitarianism to redemption and a sense of overwhelming wealth. "No greater curse was ever placed upon man," he lamented, "than the ownership of real estate in excess of what is absolutely needed." But unlike later foundation donors, tax avoidance and personal vanity did not taint his philanthropy. Conceptualized in 1913, four years before federal revenue acts allowed charitable deductions from personal income, the Brackenridge Foundation was not the result of a business decision to decrease tax liability. In fact, assessments on the wealthy, resulting from the Sixteenth Amendment (1913) to the U.S. Constitution, were relatively minuscule at the time. Private or corporate financial advantage, then, did not spur Brackenridge to give away his fortune. Nor was the fund created to glamorize and promote its founder's name. Not until after his death in 1920 and the resolution of the four-year lawsuit was the title Brackenridge Foundation attached to the simple trust agreement he had provided in his will.[16]

Despite the malicious gossip and negative criticism, Brackenridge died a respected and esteemed man. He escaped the condemnation of other wealthy men who left behind millions of unused, available funds. "The man who dies thus rich dies disgraced," Carnegie scornfully warned, and "will pass away 'unwept, unhonored, and unsung.'" The citizens of San Antonio and Texas genuinely grieved over the demise of Brackenridge, who gave away much of his fortune "during his lifetime." Memorials canonized him as a "noble saint" and a civic steward. Tributes testified to his character, civic-mindedness, and generosity. Testimonials affirmed "his love for humanity and devotion to the cause of the downtrodden and oppressed." Editorials in the *San Antonio Express* eulogized Brackenridge as the "foremost citizen" of San Antonio and a "great benefactor" of the state. His are the "beneficences that bless," the publishers wrote, and "this state and very many people in other states will mourn his departure from among them."[17]

In 1925, almost five years after his death, the trustees of the estate at last initiated the George W. Brackenridge Foundation. Following his instructions, they specified that the income from his property would accumulate until the trust equaled his net worth before payment of individual bequests, death taxes, and administrative expenses. Thereafter, according to his wishes, all remaining funds would benefit deserving young citizens—one-half to the "Anglo-Saxon race" and one-half to the "Negro race"—in obtaining an education or "for their moral or intellectual advancement."[18]

In both his private giving and organized philanthropy, education received the lion's share of his largess—and for good reason. During the Gilded Age, contributions to institutions for the "fit" exemplified acceptable benefactions for "men of means." Contrary to antebellum "benevolent ladies and Christian gentlemen" who personally labored with those of lesser means, modern philanthropists were to "bestow not befriend," according to historian Kathleen D. McCarthy. Rather than supporting traditional charities such as orphanages and asylums, they endowed great universities, established medical colleges, and funded research institutes. Vanderbilt, Johns Hopkins, and the University of Chicago were examples of their munificence, serving both as personal monuments to the donors and public gifts to the community.[19]

Within this milieu, Brackenridge also embraced "benefactions of an educational nature," but on a more modest scale. A scholar by instinct, he accepted as axiomatic the Jeffersonian premise that education produced a more responsible citizenry. Bemoaning the fact that his own formal training had been interrupted, he compensated by avidly reading books, engaging in lively debates, and, in the process, becoming a self-educated man. Brackenridge further demonstrated his commitment to higher learning by serving as regent to the University of Texas for more than twenty-five years. Former U.T. president Vinson reminisced in 1940 that during his tenure he always stressed the word "University," rather than "Texas," as if to underscore the importance of the former. Moreover, in 1917, in response to a veto by Governor James E. Ferguson of the school's biennial appropriations bill, he offered to underwrite its expenses out of his own private funds. For Brackenridge, then, education represented the best means for "the aspiring," especially young people who "had their life before them," to rise, improve themselves, and achieve economic and social mobility.[20]

Typical of many privately funded organizations, intimate friends and business associates composed the first Brackenridge Foundation board of directors, who, in turn, mapped out its governing policies. Meeting quarterly, the members included attorneys Thomas H. Franklin and Leroy G. Denman, newspaperman Frank G. Huntress, and loyal employees and friends Thomas Davis Anderson, M. C. Judson, and Sidney E. Mezes. Because Brackenridge never married and the foundation was a posthumous creation, no descendants or family members served as trustees. The first governing board then articulated its funding guidelines, designating grants only to educational institutions within the state of Texas, thereby avoiding onerous state inheritance taxes of up to twenty percent on the transfer of property to the trust. They further specified that foundation money would support students, not buildings or other infrastructure, and all requests should be written and delivered to the grant office. Recipients would then be selected "without discrimination as to race or religion." While applications by individuals received consideration, most proposals originated from the trustees themselves—a common occurrence in Texas foundations—working in partnership with public schools and local universities.[21]

For the first few decades of its existence (1925–63), as the trust recovered from its expensive litigation, the Brackenridge Foundation administered a revolving student loan program. This decision permitted the board members to carry out immediately the charitable and educational wishes of its donor, without ignoring his directions for full funding based on net worth at time of his death. The trustees also continued one of Brackenridge's little-known practices of lending money for education in exchange for a written agreement stating: "When convenient I promise to pay." Although such casual promissory notes were nonbinding and legally uncollectible, Brackenridge considered them "the best of securities," and the board upheld the custom. As a result of these loans, the trustees contended, many worthy students across the state were able to continue their studies.[22]

In addition to this program, the Brackenridge Foundation provided grants and scholarships not only to Anglo Texans, but also to black students throughout Texas—reflecting the founder's continuing interest in minority education. Derisively accused during his lifetime of being a "Negro lover," Brackenridge believed that the only practical solution to the race problem was "to educate the Negro up to the highest citizenship he was capable." Rather than challenging the existing social relations in the Jim Crow South, which mandated "separate but equal" facilities, he worked for the betterment of both races within the segregated system. "Educational reason," according to trustee Thomas H. Franklin, was his weapon to "combat error and overthrow prejudice." He therefore applied his gifts based on the approximate ratio of Anglos to black Texans—"three-fourths to whites and one-fourth to colored." Prairie View Normal School, a black facility, was the primary recipient of his largess. After his death as the percentage of aid equalized, the trustees assisted "most, if not all, of the Negro colleges in the state." Though the scholarship program significantly boosted the number of black graduates in Texas, it also maintained the doctrine of segregated schools that had been legally in effect since 1896.[23]

Brackenridge also advocated female education. He had long supported equal rights for women, particularly endorsing the suffrage campaign waged by his sister Eleanor, president of the Equal Franchise Society in San Antonio. Consequently, he liberally contributed money to many traditional and nontraditional female endeavors: financing the Women's Building at the U.T. Galveston medical branch, donating funds for a school of home economics, and establishing a loan program for coeds to study medicine, law, and architecture. Brackenridge also encouraged women to pursue professional teaching careers within the university system.[24]

Largely overlooked by Brackenridge, however, were the Mexican Americans in San Antonio, many who had been pushed from their homeland during the Mexican Revolution (1910). Barrios in the city, characterized by urban blight and human squalor, swelled with immigrants seeking a safe haven and unskilled work. Latino schools, like their black counterparts, were also substandard. While surely aware of the large Tejano community in the city, he left scant record to their plight. A product of the slave culture, the Jim Crow South, and the suffrage movement, Brackenridge focused instead much of his philanthropy toward blacks and women. He believed that these two groups, of which he was most familiar, had been denied both legal rights and equal opportunities. "Benefactions of an educational nature," therefore, would do much to equalize the prevailing social conditions.[25]

By 1963, after thirty-eight years, the trustees gradually phased out the student loan program, creating in its place the Brackenridge scholarship program. This new initiative provided a four-year financial grant to one or more graduates, regardless of sex or race, from each public high school in Bexar County. Prospective scholars competed "only against their classmates," and not against those from wealthier, higher-performing districts. As a result, students from lower socioeconomic classes could attend college, including many first-generation Mexican Americans, thereby correcting an earlier oversight.[26]

During its first fifty years, the Brackenridge Foundation, a mid-size philanthropic institution with assets of approximately $5.1 million in 1970, shunned the "routine and customary" and adopted a willingness to experiment. As attorney and board member Gilbert M. Denman Jr. wrote: "The foundation has not limited itself to the safe and the sane, but continues to seek out the untried, the new, and the more imaginative in educational opportunities." Exercising a freer hand than those in the public sector, the trustees believed that by risking possible failure they could fund projects rejected or neglected by traditional government agencies—one of the hallmarks of private philanthropy. For example, the Brackenridge Foundation sponsored numerous pilot projects, including a study hall program for potential dropouts, a bilingual experiment for preschoolers, and a library plan for purchasing Spanish language books. In addition, the trustees underwrote a cultural arts curriculum targeting impoverished children, an innovative safety program for elementary students, and instructional support for mentally retarded and handicapped children.[27]

Yet such experimental use of private wealth for the public good drew criticism. Some complained that such modern initiatives sidestepped time-honored good causes and did not always represent a legitimate use of tax-exempt funds. Others suggested that they constituted disguised attempts by elites to exercise "intellectual hegemony" and thereby influence public policy. And still others worried that private funding of nontraditional programs was potentially wasteful and disregarded donor intent. Nonetheless, many of these programs served as privately funded prototypes, without which much of the social legislation of President Lyndon B. Johnson's Great Society would have been impossible.

George W. Brackenridge, as the first modern Texas philanthropist who established the state's oldest foundation, was an archetypal turn-of-the-century benefactor. As a model civic steward, he sought socially acceptable ways to redistribute his surplus income and accomplish "far-reaching good." He achieved his goal by pro-viding deserving students with financial assistance, aiding Brackenridge scholars to enroll in institutions of higher learning, and funding academic programs that oth-erwise would have been neglected. But his magnanimity was not without rancor, at times eliciting accusations of "tainted money," elitism, and social control. Further-more, his acceptance of the "Gospel of Wealth," Social Darwinism, and racial segre-gation clearly marked him as a quintessential, Gilded Age "man of means," who leveraged his private wealth for the public good within the cultural context of his times. Brackenridge pioneered the movement toward organized philanthropy in the state, and as such served as "a patron saint" to Texas students and a model for all other wealthy Texans to follow.[28]

T W O

CHARITY BEGINS AT HOME
George Bannerman Dealey and the Creation of
The Dallas Foundation, 1929

O N FEBRUARY 27, 1946, THE LEAD STORY of the *Dallas Morning News* announced that George Bannerman Dealey, newspaper publisher and widely acclaimed "dean of the Texas press," had died quietly at his residence the previous day. Emblazoned across the front page in bold, two-inch headlines was the grim news: "G. B. DEALEY, 86, PUBLISHER OF THE NEWS, DIES." Numerous encomiums filled eight columns of print. Moving testimonials from Dallas businessmen, friends, and citizens expressed admiration for his unflagging efforts to transform a frontier town into a modern metropolis. Profuse tributes from state and national leaders attested to his seventy-two years of continuous newspaper service, as well as to his civic and philanthropic endeavors. Speaker of the House Sam Rayburn characterized him as "truly one of the builders of Texas," and state Governor Coke Stevenson considered Dealey a pioneer who "believed profoundly" in Texas. Woodall Rodgers, Dallas mayor, praised him as "one of our greatest civic inspirations for half a century." More than anything else, the *Dallas Morning News* concluded, he had remained deeply committed to the welfare of others, applying his personal philosophy, which was supposedly borrowed from Davy Crockett, to his many endeavors: "Be sure you're right, then go ahead." And he did.[1]

Of medium height and build with frosted hair and a matching, manicured mustache, Dealey embodied the spirit of modern America—immigration, urbanization, and expansion—with its unparalleled opportunities for wealth accumulation. Born on September 18, 1859, in Manchester, England, he immigrated with his parents to Texas, arriving in Galveston in 1870. Beginning four years later with the local newspaper for three dollars a week, the young entrepreneur quickly advanced from office boy to mailing clerk and then from traveling agent to branch manager. Acutely aware of the growing settlements in North Texas and eager to increase newspaper circulation, Dealey, at the behest of his employer, Colonel A. H. Belo, later founded the *Dallas Morning News* on October 1, 1885, and immediately became its business manager. For the next thirty-five years he excelled—even prospered—exercising increasing power as vice president, general manager, and president of the Belo Corporation, the parent company. Then in 1926, Dealey and his associates purchased controlling interest in the news enterprise, which now included three newspapers, an almanac, and a radio station. Although never a multimillionaire by Gilded Age stan-

George B. Dealey. Courtesy the Dallas Historical Society.

dards, he consolidated his media conglomerate and thereby joined the ranks of the wealthy class in early-twentieth-century Texas.[2]

Dealey, publisher of the *Dallas Morning News,* not only founded and guided "Texas' oldest business institution" but also championed a variety of charitable and community activities. As a progressive businessman, he supported broad public improvements in Dallas, most notably flood control levees along the Trinity River, paved streets, and pure drinking water. An official of the Cleaner Dallas League and the American Planning and Civic Association, Dealey was a tireless advocate of the Kessler Plan as well, which applied long-range municipal planning to haphazard city growth. Believing that education was essential to democracy and that newspapers were "citizens of the community served," he marshaled the vast resources of the *Dallas Morning News* in 1911 to promote higher education by establishing Southern Methodist University; he continued this crusading pattern repeatedly throughout his career by serving as the first president of the Family Welfare Bureau, director of the Richmond Freeman Memorial Clinic, president of the United Charities of Dallas, and honorary vice president of the National Housing Association. In 1922, captivated by "the cavalcade of Texas history," he founded and became life president of the Dallas Historical Society—later designated as the custodian of the Hall of State. He even constructed a replica of the Alamo at Fair Park on two separate occasions so that residents of North Texas would have the opportunity to view that historic landmark. However, one of his most significant contributions was the creation in 1929 of the Dallas Community Trust, now The Dallas Foundation—the oldest community, grant-making organization in Texas—that was dedicated to "the well being of mankind in the Dallas area."[3]

By the twentieth century the concept of community—a shared sense of place and belonging—was a well-established trait in the American character. John Winthrop had established the earliest blueprint in 1630 by describing "a city on a hill" in his sermon, "A Modell of Christian Charity." This Calvinist ideal of mutual assistance ensured the survival of the early colony through civic stewardship. Alexis de Tocqueville in 1835 further discerned the loyalties of citizens toward their communities.

By forming an immense variety of associations, he wrote, "Americans of all ages, all stations in life, and all types of disposition," voluntarily helped each other. Succeeding generations, regardless of their religious affiliation, ethnic background, or socioeconomic level, also engaged in charitable practices through benevolent groups, voluntary associations, and mutual aid societies. Community building through philanthropy, as Professor Arthur Schlesinger Sr. noted in 1953, was "another of the distinguishing marks of the American way."[4]

Texans were also concerned citizens who built communities and promoted philanthropic endeavors. They formed benevolent societies, fraternal groups, and charitable institutions to help one another cope with a raw, hostile environment. The rise of urban Texas and its steady stream of hopeful settlers moving from rural areas to major cities led a few civic leaders to envision a broader, more permanent vehicle to address their problems, particularly those neglected or underserved by private charities or federal aid. Thus, with a typical Progressive era emphasis on reform and efficiency, Dallas and similar towns organized community foundations with a strong identification to local needs.[5]

Beginning early in the twentieth century the community foundation movement offered a distinct alternative to the larger, national endowments created by industrialists Carnegie and Rockefeller. In 1914 Judge Frederick H. Goff, a lawyer and banker, founded the oldest known operating model in Cleveland, Ohio. Concerned about the rigidity of giving carried out through charitable trusts, especially the practice of mortmain, or "the dead hand," he conceived of a plan to assure the safe, flexible use of such gifts. "How fine it would be," Goff stated, "if a person could say: 'Here is a large sum of money that I shall no longer need.'" He then suggested that the individual donate the surplus funds to a new philanthropic organization, guided by civic leaders, which would then determine "what should be done with this sum to make it most useful for people of each succeeding generation." Gradually the idea spread, Yale scholar Peter Dobkin Hall noted, proving particularly attractive to midsize urban centers with "strong, elite-dominated reformist political cultures." Rather than a private, general-purpose foundation funded by a wealthy individual or family, this new form of philanthropy consolidated many large and small gifts to benefit a particular city or region. Board members, composed of public officials and community leaders, served limited unpaid terms, thereby replacing the self-perpetuating bodies that controlled independent private organizations. With a more localized focus, community foundations also readily responded to the immediate needs and pressing concerns of their citizens. Equally important, with urban problems in a constant state of flux, they provided greater grant-making flexibility with funds that were not yoked to donor intent. Each generation determined how the money should be spent, thus eliminating the spectral reach of "the dead hand"—obsolete trust funds created in perpetuity—as well as the cy pres doctrine, which was the legal procedure to recover those monies for useful purposes.[6]

Community foundations also offered powerful inducements to donors seeking a respected and reliable place for their philanthropic funds. If desired, wealthy contributors designated the intent of their gift and selected an individual or family name for the fund. To avoid the pitfalls of perpetual endowments, however, they surrendered ultimate financial control to trusted experts whom, when necessary, channeled their money to new and more relevant purposes. For example, when community requirements changed or emergencies arose, trustees were free to redirect the funds to meet the greatest human needs. At the same time, donors of more modest means, whose individual gifts normally would not accrue significant income, pooled their resources with others for greater investment potential. As a result, they enjoyed the advantages of a diverse portfolio that minimized risks and maximized returns, while providing more substantial grants. Moreover, recipients of such assistance resided in the home community, thereby satisfying donor intent and channeling charitable dollars back into the local economy. With the aid of familiar and reputable local institutions, the trust also provided all legal, organizational, and financial services, thus freeing the benefactors of additional administrative and operational costs. In contrast to conventional private philanthropic organizations, community foundations, which were reclassified as publicly funded charities in 1964, increasingly qualified for higher tax deductions—another attractive incentive to sway potential clients. In short, community foundations, according to former Ford Foundation staffer and scholar Waldemar Nielsen, were "a great invention."[7]

By the early twentieth century, Dallas, like many cities in the Midwest and South, had developed a civic culture receptive to the creation of a community foundation. With the city emerging as a mid-size commercial center, boasting a population of 158,976 in 1920—and an even larger metropolitan area—young, public-spirited entrepreneurs eagerly sought to capitalize on the economic good times, thus stimulating urban development. Further, they shared a commitment to progress through efficient government and better public services, what historian George B. Tindall called "business progressivism," thereby indirectly subsidizing their own self-interests. Typically, these Dallas boosters implemented their vision using such devices as municipal reform, civic organizations, and voluntary associations. Their efforts resulted in the establishment of the Kessler Plan for a citywide blueprint, a Dallas Citizens' Council—a forerunner to the Chamber of Commerce—and a Community Chest, a federated, charitable giving campaign. In the process, they helped transform Dallas from a turn-of-the-century regional outpost to a self-styled "Queen City of the Southwest" by 1950. Dealey, the tremendously visible publisher of the *Dallas Morning News,* served as a rallying point for this enterprising group.[8]

Beginning in 1920 Dealey became aware, and then convinced, of the merit of community foundations. As a wealthy steward who believed that newspaper publishers should "involve themselves wholesomely in public and civic affairs," he immediately grasped the import of this new philanthropic institution and its potential to achieve "incomparable good" for Dallas. Moreover, he recognized its many advantages to "democratize philanthropy" by expanding the number of donors while assuring that their charitable funds would be of lasting benefit. Dealey frequently met with city leaders to discuss this concept and solicit their opinions, but he did not actively promote the cause. Not until two years later, after businessman George Waverley Briggs presented a paper on the topic to the Critic Club, an exclusive fifteen-member fraternity of Dallas leaders, did he openly endorse the concept. The speech, "Should Dallas Establish a Public Foundation or Community Trust as a Means of Solving its Charity Problems and Promoting its Cultural and Civic Growth?" persuaded him, more than anything else, of its "sane, sound modern method of making bequests." Thereafter, Dealey, ever the crusader and visionary, continually championed and publicized the issue in hopes of winning its acceptance by Dallas residents.[9]

The Briggs proposal, which urged "the establishment and ultimate usefulness of a Community Trust in Dallas," elicited considerable interest, discussion, and eventual endorsement by the Critic Club. These urban elites believed that Dallas had suffered from a lack of public benefactions that more fortunate cities enjoyed. They therefore supported any meaningful avenue of "practical service to humanity" that would profit the community and encompass all levels of giving. The progressive

The Critic Club, ca. 1928. Courtesy the Dallas Historical Society.

businessmen also valued large-scale, organized philanthropy, which eliminated haphazard giving and standardized charitable practices, thereby achieving greater efficiency. After prolonged deliberation they too endorsed the creation of a community foundation in Dallas and appointed a committee of five—Chairman George Waverley Briggs, L. M. Dabney, M. M. Crane, J. K. Hexter, and G. B. Dealey—to test the idea, educate the public, and build a base of support.[10]

From 1922 to 1929 Dealey, together with the Critic Club members, maintained a continual public campaign for the project. They frequently debated the topic among themselves and other prominent citizens, at times eliciting spirited exchanges. Increasingly, the committee members solicited the assistance of financial institutions, trust companies, and civic organizations in Dallas by outlining the advantages of a community foundation to all concerned. With equal success they sought the endorsement of the Chamber of Commerce, an organization traditionally charged with civic and charitable concerns. But most importantly, Dealey enlisted the considerable circulation, advertising, and editorial powers of the *Dallas Morning News* to win support for the plan. As biographer Ernest Sharpe explained, the publisher developed a successful formula for his many crusades: "Start something good, call in the city leaders, let them take charge, support them with the *News,* give them the credit, play the role of coordinator, and keep working at it."[11]

On February 18, 1929, Briggs, now president of the Dallas Chamber of Commerce, appointed a community trust committee to study "the material gathered from authoritative sources" and to prepare a brief report. The members were aware that the A. H. Belo Corporation, along with the Times Herald Printing Company that published the *Daily Times Herald* and the Dallas Dispatch Company that printed the *Dallas Dispatch,* had previously drawn up a legal instrument; they therefore agreed to forge a coalition. Meeting with Belo attorney Eugene P. Locke on June 21, the participants examined the trust agreement, which defined its charitable purposes in the broadest terms possible, and suggested several revisions. Then, with assurances that the final draft would reflect their concerns, the committee unanimously approved the proposal and recommended its acceptance. On June 25 the Dallas Chamber of Commerce joined with Dealey, now seventy years old, and the other charter sponsors in this endeavor. The Dallas Community Trust, later renamed The Dallas Foundation, became a reality.[12]

Beginning in 1929 Dealey, although engaged in a host of business and civic activities, indefatigably advanced the cause of this new community philanthropy for Dallas citizens. Convinced that such a project required both publicity and sponsorship—an innovation designed to capture public attention—he unleashed an escalating media campaign through his newspaper columns. The power of the press, the publisher announced, could "help push along the idea of the Dallas Community Trust." As in all Dealey campaigns, his modus operandi, that of printing testimonials from individuals associated with the movement, appeared with regularity. Dealey also wrote "literally hundreds of letters to the members of the Bench and Bar of Dallas," Briggs recalled, requesting their opinions for publication. For example, he contacted such leading officials as Robert Lee Bobbitt, Texas attorney general, who endorsed the plan as "the most practical, efficient and far-reaching organization of its kind." Furthermore, he sent its legal instrument to prominent lawyers, government officials, and leading journalists throughout the state for their approval. Upon receiving their responses, he published "one or two letters a day." And at company expense he produced hundreds of Dallas Community Trust brochures and then disseminated them to potential donors and bank customers. By unrelentingly keeping the issue before the public, Dealey, now in his seventies, hoped to see The Dallas Foundation firmly established before he "passed out of the picture."[13]

Throughout the summer and fall of 1929, the foundation sponsors also initiated a selection process for the first board of governors, which was no easy task. Particularly problematic was the language of the organizing agreement. The proposal stipulated that the seven members must be Dallas County residents who were neither public officeholders nor candidates. They had to be "matured men or women, outstanding in the community, well traveled, [and] of broad experience with the world." Furthermore, they must possess impeccable attributes, being "sympathetic with all types and classes of people, tolerant of the views of others, of recognized probity, sound judgment and philanthropic disposition." For any alleged misconduct or "unfavorable public criticism or notoriety," which might minimize public opinion and reflect unfavorably on the trust, they must resign immediately. Such stringent requirements, the founders believed, deterred any taint of internal corruption or public distrust. On February 28, 1930, after months of screening, the sponsor representatives assembled at the Adolphus Hotel and unanimously elected seven highly qualified business leaders—Chairman Edgar L. Flippen, Secretary Frank L. McNeny, Edwy R. Brown, John H. McDonough, Edward T. Moore, Leroy R. Munger, and Edward Titche—to complete the first board of governors of The Dallas Foundation.[14]

Because of the unique public character of community foundations, the rules governing The Dallas Foundation board differed significantly from those of other philanthropic institutions. Unlike private, independent foundations with interlocking, self-perpetuating boards of trustees often composed of family members, these appointive officials served limited terms—without compensation. When vacancies occurred, the chairman of the board of governors designated a nominating committee of three to five members, rather than the donors as in other private foundations, to select a slate of candidates. If, however, they failed to fill the open positions, persons holding key posts in the district courts and public agencies would choose the replacements. In addition, as a fund distribution committee they served solely as a grant-making body for "public charitable purposes," while entrusting the management of assets to leading local banks. Such safeguards, Dealey and the others believed, ensured the high standing of board members, instilled public confidence within the community, and avoided much of the censure directed at institutional philanthropy—dynastic control, self-aggrandizement, and private misconduct.[15]

Despite attempts to assure open, broadly representative grant-making decisions, the first board of governors of The Dallas Foundation was remarkably homogenous—reflecting the socioeconomic climate of early-twentieth-century Texas. Of the original charter members all were white, Anglo-Saxon, elite businessmen, while a majority—five of the seven trustees—were Protestant. Each held a position of prominence within the Dallas commercial community. For instance, one was a president of a petroleum company, another owned an automobile dealership, and still another operated a retail store. In a city where women outnumbered men in 1930 by approximately 8,000, no females secured an appointment. Despite having recently acquired the vote in 1920, women—constrained both by law and custom—exercised limited financial and political power; instead, they maintained active memberships in civic clubs and charitable organizations as their access to the public sphere. Minorities such as African Americans and Hispanics, composing approximately fifteen and three percent of the population respectively, also were conspicuous by their absence. Few opportunities, inadequate education, and pernicious segregation consigned them to low-wage labor and service positions. As a result, with such a narrowly defined board, the first governing body of The Dallas Foundation contained no members from these historically underrepresented and discriminated groups. The disbursal of charitable funds in early-twentieth-century Dallas therefore hinged on a definition of community needs determined by those with the greatest resources, namely elite, white, mostly Protestant males. Despite such "philanthropic paternalism," which characterized most grant-making organizations of the era, The Dallas Foundation nevertheless represented a new, more publicly responsible method to allocate surplus funds for charitable purposes.[16]

With the grant-making function separate from the management of assets, The Dallas Foundation relied on members of the Dallas Clearing House Association, composed of neighborhood banks and trust companies, to serve as multiple agents for the community money. As incorporated institutions, they received and supervised donor gifts, then issued quarterly reports to the board of governors, providing an accounting both of the principal and the income. Thus, the involvement of respected and reliable local financial organizations provided another attractive factor to family members who sought to transfer their wealth to support charitable causes.[17]

The Dallas Foundation faced many early obstacles. Created just four months before the onset of the Great Depression, it suffered from the devastating effects of the crash. With many fortunes diminished, the ongoing economic uncertainty discouraged philanthropic giving and eroded confidence in banks. "In these precarious times," board member Edwin Kiest lamented, "a man does not know what his estate will amount to at his death." Private Dallas agencies, such as United Charities and the Community Chest, shouldered the burdens of the poor and unemployed until their funds were exhausted. Wealthy donors then necessarily shifted in favor of increased government action under New Deal programs. Little wonder that Dealey, concerned and apprehensive, wrote New York Community Trust officer Ralph

Hayes in January, 1931, that "there have been no contributions of any sort yet." Nor would conditions readily improve. For example, the 1935 Tax Act with its "soak-the-rich" progressive assessments on the wealthy also contributed to further inactivity. The net effect of the increased taxation was a decrease in charitable giving, especially to community foundations under public control. As Wilmer Shields Rich of the Council on Community Foundations observed, the depression "saw a lull in the development of new community foundations" as well as the "failure to grow of many already established."[18]

Despite the sluggishness of donations, Dealey remained optimistic. Like many other Texans, he refused to believe that the economic crisis would be long lasting. After all, the *Dallas Morning News* during the early 1930s, even with losses in advertising revenues, had continued to meet its payroll; and President Herbert Hoover, perceiving the events rather simplistically in 1930, had calmly reassured the nation that "we have now passed the worst," and "prosperity was just around the corner." Dealey, who had survived four national depressions and recessions during his career, seemingly agreed. He therefore applied the president's positive attitude to the infant Dallas Foundation by brashly proclaiming in January, 1931, that it was not "a flop." As a skillful civic leader, Dealey understood that the early years of such a project were formative ones. "A community trust is necessarily of slow growth," he asserted, particularly during hard times. Refusing to become dispirited, he was further encouraged by the board of governors and financial officers who announced that several Dallas citizens had already written bequests to the trust. Plans to "liven the interest" by sending out informational literature to bank customers, Dealey confidently concluded, would help "push the project earnestly from now on." Then, in keeping with his personal philosophy to "keep working at it," especially on worthwhile projects, he glowingly predicted that the future of the new foundation was "exceedingly bright."[19]

Dealey was not disappointed. On March 21, 1935, The Dallas Foundation recorded its first bequest from Sigmund Mayer, a local retailer. Described as "a reticent, modest man and a bachelor," Mayer had immigrated to the United States from Germany as a teenager. He joined the department store business of Mayer and Schmidt, launched by his brother Abraham in Nacogdoches, then moved to Tyler, and finally settled in Dallas. By 1929 Mayer, now working for the Titche-Goettinger department store, enjoyed both commercial and financial success. Equally important, he was known for his "kind and generous nature . . . a friend to former and present employees of Mayer and Schmidt."[20]

Through his contact with Edward Titche, a member of the board of governors, Mayer became aware of The Dallas Foundation as a worthy recipient of his funds, "fitted to changing conditions" rather than "tied to an outmoded need." As a result, when Mayer died in 1934 at age sixty-nine he bequeathed $10,000 to the new fund. Considered a large sum at the time—comparable to about $130,000 in 2004—his bequest initiated the unrestricted use fund, thereby rescuing the moribund foundation. Five years later on April 13, 1939, the board of governors authorized its first grant of $1,000 to rebuild the West Dallas Social Center that was destroyed by fire and to construct a much-needed playground in the neighborhood. From the charred ruins rose a new, brick community center, which became a focus for neighborhood activities—a gift made possible by Sigmund Mayer. Thus, by the end of the decade, Briggs cogently observed that The Dallas Foundation was now "a going concern."[21]

During the 1940s, as the depression slowly receded into memory and the nation mobilized for war, The Dallas Foundation underwent significant changes and growth. On August 28, 1942, the first amendment to the trust agreement in more than thirteen years altered its name from the Dallas Community Trust to The Dallas Foundation, thus avoiding confusion with another charitable organization, the Dallas Community Chest. Then, due to wartime demands, followed by postwar prosperity, Dallas population soared by approximately fifty percent, thereby boosting bequests and gifts of varying sizes to over $117,000. In turn, The Dallas Foundation grants increased to approximately $25,000 by mid-century. The deaths of eighty-seven-year-old Dealey on February 26, 1946, and Eugene P. Locke one week later at age sixty-three, signified the end of an era. With the passing both of the "founder and designer" of the first community trust in Texas, two new funds enlarged its resources. Dealey bequeathed $10,000 from his estate to the foundation, while Locke left an insurance policy valued at more than $4,000. As a result, The Dallas Foundation revived to meet the needs of a changing society.[22]

In many ways the history of the creation of The Dallas Foundation reflected the story of urban Texas and the vision of George Bannerman Dealey. As the state became less rural during the early twentieth century, cities such as Dallas benefited through population growth and economic stimulation. The Great Depression, the New Deal, and World War II accelerated that process. Such phenomenal expansion brought attendant social ills and demands for improved municipal services. Even the emergency programs of President Franklin D. Roosevelt, which implemented many of the protections that an urban-industrial society required, did not fully ameliorate its deep-seated problems. Progressive businessmen such as Dealey, who sought rational, efficient ways to enhance their communities and advance urban development, therefore became reform activists and civic boosters. By 1929, as the community trust movement reached a total of approximately fifty such organizations nationwide, The Dallas Foundation was simply "an idea whose time had come." It found its most effective spokesman in George Bannerman Dealey, who became convinced of its merits, and then "proceeded ahead."[23]

THREE

NEW DEAL DONOR
Jesse H. Jones and the Houston Endowment, Inc., 1937

"NEXT TO THE PRESIDENT," the *Saturday Evening Post* reported on November 30, 1940, "no man in the government and probably in the United States wields greater powers" than Jesse Holman Jones. Although he neither sought nor held elective office, Jones, as director of the Reconstruction Finance Corporation—a depression-era agency created by President Herbert Hoover—had dispensed more than $35 billion to banks, railroads, farms, and industry over a ten-year period. Rivaling the political and financial clout of banker J. P. Morgan, who rescued the nation from bankruptcy in 1895–96, Jones created his own personal fiefdom and, according to historian James S. Olson, single-handedly "saved capitalism." In 1940, President Franklin D. Roosevelt appointed him secretary of commerce, in addition to his position as federal loan administrator, constituting what many critics considered "a fourth branch of government." Only the strength of Jones's character and the severity of the national emergency, Republican Senator Robert A. Taft observed, justified such an "extraordinary precedent." Then, with the advent of World War II, Roosevelt conferred even greater authority on Jones, expanding his responsibilities to include additional government agencies, such as the Export-Import Bank, the Patent Office, and the Census Bureau, as well as increasing his jurisdiction over seven wartime corporations. When Jones sometimes stretched the limits of his already considerable power, the president mockingly referred to him as "Jesus H. Jones." As Vice President John Nance Garner counseled his friend: "Jesse, Congress has given you powers which no man ought to have, and I know of no one but you who could get them."[1]

The impact of Jones on his region was no less immense. As a progressive, Tennessee-born businessman who vaulted onto the national stage in the 1920s, he embodied many values of the South—loyalty, honor, and tradition—as well as an instinctive distrust of "northern colonizers." Resenting the impersonal control exercised by eastern corporations over southern industries, Jones, as a New Deal administrator, labored to reverse such exploitation. For instance, he utilized his considerable federal powers to convince railroad executives and other company directors to relocate their main offices away from Wall Street and nearer their regional operating centers. "I'll lend you the money," he proffered, "but you'll have to move out of New York." Close friend Judge James A. Elkins once observed about the Houstonian: Jones provided the South with "greater recognition" than any other individual in its history.[2]

Jesse H. Jones. From the *San Antonio Light* Collection, no. 0067-N, courtesy U.T. Institute of Texan Cultures at San Antonio.

At the same time, Jones manifested a personal allegiance to his adopted state of Texas and especially his hometown of Houston. Influenced early in life by Baptist minister Russell H. Conwell, who repeatedly delivered his "Acres of Diamonds" lecture to nationwide audiences, Jones subscribed to its convincing message. "Greatness," Conwell contended, "consists in doing great deeds with little means . . . in the private ranks of life—in helping one's fellows, benefiting one's neighborhood, [and] in blessing one's own city and state." Accordingly, Jones became one of Houston's most vigorous boosters, promoting local opportunities for growth and modernization that not only profited the community, but also "Jones interests" as well. For example, in 1911 he became convinced that the "Bayou City," located fifty miles inland from the Gulf of Mexico, required access to the sea for its economic future. Several Texas coastal cities at the time competed for commercial dominance; Jones decided to join a delegation to raise funds for a deepwater canal that would accommodate oceangoing vessels. In 1914 the Houston Ship Channel opened, thereby attracting dozens of new industries to Texas, as well as internationalizing the port of Houston. "I always said that Houston would be the 'Chicago of the South,'" he later boasted. Jones accomplished another impressive feat in 1928. He successfully lobbied the Democratic National Committee to choose his city for the presidential convention by promising personally to build a 25,000-seat meeting hall—a tour de force he accomplished within a matter of months! Thus, by hosting the event—the first southern city to do so since the Civil War—and then gaining appointment as Reconstruction Finance Corporation director in 1932, Jones was able to focus national attention on Houston. As a result, the city quickly became the largest in the state, and, by 1940, with a population of 384,514, it emerged as the fulcrum of the Texas economy—much to the credit of Jesse Jones, the indisputable "Mr. Houston."[3]

Much like Franklin Roosevelt, who was the privileged son of a prominent Hyde Park family, Jones owed much of his phenomenal success to his birthright and talent. Born on April 5, 1874, near Springfield, Tennessee, to a prosperous tobacco farmer and his wife, William Hasque and Laura Anna Jones, he lived in a comfort-able house whose "mantels were of marble and doorknobs of silver." Husky and broad shouldered, Jones attended public school until the eighth grade, then joined his father in the family business. In 1893, however, he rejected an opportunity to at-tend college, declaring that "arithmetic was the only subject that interested him." Yet he yearned for "a better way of making a living than tobacco raising." Consequently, he moved to Dallas and worked in a lumberyard owned by his uncle, Martin T. Jones, advancing quickly from bookkeeper to superintendent and ultimately to manager. In 1898, at age twenty-four, Jones transferred to Houston to manage his uncle's estate, valued in excess of $1 million. With uncanny entrepreneurial in-stincts, as well as strong kinship and business ties, he bought his first lumberyard and launched the South Texas Lumber Company to build small, low-cost homes. In 1905 Jones also formed the Southern Loan and Investment Company to provide affordable mortgages to working-class families. After acquiring sixty-five more lum-ber properties to meet the growing demand for construction, thirty-two-year-old Jones joined the millionaire class in one of the fastest growing industries in the state.[4]

For the next quarter century (1906–31), Jones demonstrated unusual business acumen and gradually consolidated his commercial empire. Eschewing the typically unstable Houston commodities of cotton, chemicals, and oil, he favored other sound investments with tangible assets. "If a man wants to get rich, he can do it with things on the face of the earth," he explained, "things which can be plainly seen, without speculating on what is hidden underneath." Jones therefore sold his sawmill interests to pursue his real passions—building, real estate, and finance. In quick succession he shrewdly purchased land tracts in downtown Houston and then constructed the nine-story Bristol Hotel in 1907, the ten-story Texas Company Building in 1908, and the ten-story Chronicle Building in 1910. Thereafter, he tersely stated, "I never stopped building." Careful never to place his name on any of these edifices, he proceeded to erect more than fifty skyscrapers, including his most ambitious project in 1929, the thirty-seven story Gulf Building—"the tallest build-ing south of St. Louis." But Jones, "as much of an empire builder as James J. Hill or Cecil Rhodes," according to Charles G. Dawes, former vice president and RFC chairman, did not limit his ventures to Houston; he constructed office and apart-ment buildings in Dallas, Fort Worth, Memphis, and New York City. "I build in New York," he explained, "because, in my opinion, there is no safer investment than New York real estate." By 1931 he had assiduously acquired a diverse network of business enterprises, including ownership of the National Bank of Commerce, Bankers Mortgage Company, the *Houston Chronicle,* the *Houston Post-Dispatch,* ra-dio station KTRH, and the Commerce Company—a Texas corporation. As Jones glowingly boasted: "I played business all over the board and built a city."[5]

As a prominent member of Houston's ruling elite by the 1930s, Jones was known as "a large man with a large ego." Possessing a striking mien—six feet, three inches, over 220 pounds with silver hair, black brows, and thin, compressed lips—he was limned to be "as handsome as an arrow collar advertisement." So distinctive was his appearance that media stories personified him as the stereotypical "tall Texan"— strong, self-reliant, and rich. These larger-than-life qualities frequently carried over into his business practices, where he often planned in a big way and invariably received commitments for more loans than he needed. Ambitious, energetic, at times even autocratic, Jones prided himself with owning the biggest newspaper, the highest building, the richest bank—and residing in "the largest state in the Union." In 1937 he even designed and erected "the tallest man-made memorial in the world," the San Jacinto Monument, eclipsing the Washington Monument by more than fourteen feet! As a conservative New Deal administrator, he continued this commanding role by brokering million-dollar deals, controlling important patronage, both on the state and national levels, and authorizing "more money than any man in history." Little wonder then that when he decided in 1937, along with wife Mary Gibbs Jones, to practice large-scale "wholesale philanthropy," Jones established an institution of considerable magnitude—the Houston Endowment, Inc., named for the city they called home and heralded as one of the largest in the state.[6]

The decision to institutionalize his philanthropy arose from a long-standing tradition of private charitable giving. As a youth, Jones had inherited not only his standards of good business conduct, according to biographer Bascom N. Timmons, but also his values of social responsibility. While working in the tobacco fields and warehouses, he had frequently observed numerous acts of generosity by his father. For example, the family smokehouse was always open "to those who needed a little tiding over until harvest time." Jones therefore modeled this pattern of private giving, or "retail philanthropy," by frequently dispensing numerous, often-unpublicized gifts. In 1900 his earliest donation of $100 was to help build a new church roof, but the deacons, perplexed that "he could have made enough money properly in such a short period of time," promptly returned the money. But a lack of financial resources never deterred him from supporting a worthy cause; he simply adopted a practical modus operandi: pledge the needed amount, appeal to community leaders, and then collect the necessary funds. Many times he even surpassed his own fund-raising goals, which served to spur him "to get in the [economic] class they already think [I'm] in." Consequently, as his wealth increased, his largess multiplied as well. For example, Jones frequently gave sizable monetary handouts, "big enough to choke a dog," to assuage the pride of losing athletes; he also quietly set up a trust fund for the family of Eugene Schacher, his pilot who had died in a plane crash that Jones survived. In 1923, along with several close friends, he established a $10,000-a-year trust fund to ease the financial burden of former President Woodrow Wilson. The only caveat Jones customarily proffered to the recipients was: "Don't say it's from me."[7]

The Jones family legacy of charitable giving nevertheless does not fully explain the formalization of his philanthropy. After all, the creation of the Houston Endowment was also a product of his business acumen. As a finance capitalist, Jones understood the application of sound credit, efficient management, and conservative investment.

"I never was a speculator," he remarked. "When I gambled, it was always with my surplus marbles. I never risked my shooter." Consequently, Jones adroitly managed his surplus income with the same attention to "the bottom line" as to his working capital. His years as a Washington bureaucrat had uniquely prepared him for the task of charitable grant making. As director general of the Red Cross, federal loan administrator, RFC chairman, and secretary of commerce for more than a dozen years, he had gained invaluable experience directing fund-raising, distributing essential commodities, approving loan applicants, dispensing needed credit, and opposing reckless lending practices. In tribute to his considerable financial abilities, President Roosevelt commented that Jones was "the only man in Washington who can and does say 'yes' and 'no' intelligently 24 hours a day!" Billie Mayfield, a newspaper reporter for *The Alice Echo,* also appreciated his remarkable talents, observing that "he could analyze any proposition in ten minutes with his x-ray financial eyes." Surely with such perspicacity and "keen vision," Jones did not overlook the significance of the 1935 Tax Act. Residing in Washington, D.C., and familiar with the exercise of power, he must have been aware of the effects of the new "soak-the-rich" tax assessments and five percent corporate charitable deduction on his vast holdings. A permanent philanthropic foundation with the prospects of a tax break and continued control over the "Jones interests" represented a sound investment—one that did not risk "his shooter." In 1937 Jones therefore turned to "organized philanthropy," applying his successful business formula that had built an empire and "saved capitalism" to his charitable endeavors.[8]

Motivated both by altruism and self-interest, Jones considered himself a civic steward, subscribing to many of the tenets outlined by Carnegie in his classic 1889 essay, "Wealth." Like San Antonio publisher-philanthropist George W. Brackenridge, he lived modestly as Carnegie directed, usually in one of his hotels, taking only occasional leisurely vacations while eschewing any display of extravagance or publicity. Jones also provided for the "legitimate wants" of his extended family that included a stepson, nieces, and nephews—another duty of a "man of wealth." Moreover, he contributed handsomely to loyal employees by bequeathing $300,000 to more than 2,500 workers in companies controlled by the "Jones interests." Equally important, Jones attended to the administration of his wealth "during his lifetime," much as Carnegie recommended. By establishing the Houston Endowment and conferring a broad, general purpose to its mission, he shifted from "indiscriminate charity," which often encouraged "the slothful, the drunken, the unworthy," as Carnegie believed, to "enlightened philanthropy," which earmarked gifts for the "fit," and supplied "ladders upon which the aspiring can rise."[9]

But civic stewardship held a dual obligation of money and time—a role that Jones recognized. In 1917, when President Woodrow Wilson called on him to raise funds for the American Red Cross, he had responded by personally soliciting pledges from Houstonians for more than $250,000 "without ever having a mass meeting or a working committee." Jones then accepted a two-year assignment as director general of military relief with the Red Cross. Serving as a "dollar-a-year man," he organized 50 base hospitals, recruited 145 ambulance units, and created 45 rehabilitation centers, earning the sobriquet "Big Brother to four million men in khaki." Moreover, he was indirectly responsible for supplying the Red Cross with the slogan, "Give Until It Hurts." After World War I, Jones continued his public service as a delegate to the postwar peace conferences, helping transform the Red Cross from a loose-knit group of local societies into a permanent international relief agency. Upon completion of his work in March, 1919, Jones promised Wilson "to do anything for you anywhere on a voluntary basis" and then returned home to attend to his personal affairs. This experience, which Jones considered "the greatest thing that has come to me in my entire life," provided him with his first glimpse of humanitarian service on a large scale and prepared him for a life of public service.[10]

During World War I and its aftermath Jones gradually adopted an ideology that would guide his future philanthropy. His unpaid service with the Red Cross had exposed him to the concept of the "associative state," with its emphasis on voluntarism and the private distribution of charitable funds. Originally promulgated by Herbert Hoover, a millionaire mining engineer and wartime food administrator, this model of "progressive individualism" had promoted cooperation, service, and efficiency as an alternative to state socialism or unregulated capitalism. Like other progressive businessmen of the 1920s, Jones had readily accepted these ideals, which buttressed his own personal philosophy of civic responsibility.[11]

After 1931, associational activity through personal sacrifice and business compliance proved insufficient to meet the massive challenges of the Great Depression. With more than 350,000 Texans—and millions nationwide— out of work, Jones recognized that public needs had far outpaced the capacities of individual largess. Private charities had proved wholly inadequate; local governments had exhausted their treasuries; and federal attempts to reverse the downward economic spiral had failed. The severity of the depression, he acknowledged, had changed the dynamic, thereby redefining the place of civic stewardship in an industrialized society. Henceforth, voluntarism would never occupy its previously dominant place. Instead, the federal government would play an expanded role in areas traditionally considered the province of private philanthropy.[12]

During the 1930s, with the increased incursion by big government and the devastating erosion of many Texas fortunes, the creation of private foundations necessarily waned—but did not vanish. Gradually after 1936, with rising, but unwarranted optimism that "the depression was over," as well as new legislation allowing corporate charitable deductions, several Texas funds, such as the Houston Endowment, soon became a reality. Accordingly, on April 25, 1937, the Joneses, who were childless, began plans to transfer much of their income-producing properties—newspaper, insurance, hotel, radio, and office holdings—to a new philanthropic institution in support of "any charitable, educational, or religious undertaking." Shrewd financial practices, opportunistic banking buyouts, and "aggressive lending to the oil industry" by Jones during the depression had garnered profits to help fund the new philanthropy. On September 25, 1937, with the assistance of a young lawyer, Howard Creekmore, whom Jones considered "almost as an adopted son," the donors chartered the organization with the state for fifty years as a general-purpose, nonprofit foundation. This action served to limit the financial liability of its officers and promote its tax-exempt status. Two days later the first, self-perpetuating board of trustees—F. J. Heyne, Commerce Company president; M. A. Backlund, Commercial and Industrial Life Insurance president; and W. W. Moore, Bankers Mortgage Company vice president—accepted its first gift of 10,500 shares of capital stock valued at more than $1.7 million, a sizable fortune in depression-era Texas.[13]

Understandably, as the Houston Endowment became active, it supported causes familiar to Jesse and Mary Gibbs Jones. Not initially restricted to Texas recipients, as most other private foundations in the state, the fund reflected the Joneses's unique national and global perspectives. For example, the foundation awarded its first grant from Commerce Company stock dividends, a meager twenty dollars, to the Georgia Warm Springs Foundation, which operated a therapeutic retreat frequented by Franklin Roosevelt, a polio victim. Larger grants (1937–46) to favorite institutions followed, including $139,715 to schools and colleges, $52,165 to churches, and $141,174 to miscellaneous charities. Following World War II, due to his longtime admiration of President Woodrow Wilson and his subsequent conversion to internationalism, Jones in 1945 provided a $300,000 gift to the University of Virginia for the establishment of a school of foreign affairs. This new institution, Jones stated, would provide "young Americans a livelier appreciation of the vital interests and heavy responsibilities of the United States in the outside world."[14]

The primary mission of the Houston Endowment, however, centered on providing scholarships to "worthy but poor young men and women" of all races to complete their education. Jones, a school dropout who claimed that he had read only one book in his entire life—a biography of Sam Houston—nonetheless recognized the importance of learning. "My own educational training was decidedly limited," he wrote Texas businessmen Mike Hogg and Raymond Dickson in 1924, "and I have keenly felt it a great handicap." He then resolved, along with wife Mary, who had attended college in Waco, "to assist other ambitious young men and women in equipping themselves for life's problems with a college training." As a result, by the early 1950s the foundation had established scholarships at thirty-nine colleges and universities, benefiting approximately 442 scholars each year. Recipients ranged from students attending the University of Texas and Abilene Christian College to the University of Oslo in Norway and Tuskegee Institute in Alabama. By the time of Jones's death in 1956, the foundation had aided the education of more than 4,000 students on fifty-seven campuses.[15]

Akin to their interest in education and mindful of the Carnegie model of philanthropy, the Joneses supported free libraries as well. Beginning in 1940, the Houston

Endowment generously contributed to numerous funds such as the A&M College library in College Station and the Franklin D. Roosevelt Library in Hyde Park, New York. In 1948 the foundation contributed $160,000 to build the Gibbs Memorial Library in Mexia, Texas, the birthplace of Mary Jones. Erected on the Gibbs family homestead, the library was of continuing interest to Mary, who regularly supplied books for its shelves. These institutional gifts, the Joneses believed, fulfilled their intention to benefit local communities while improving "the general condition of the people."[16]

Throughout their union, as Jesse Jones attended to his many business interests, directed the national recovery, and practiced philanthropy on a princely scale, Mary Gibbs Jones, "a patient, silver-haired woman" who was often described as "a retiring, home-loving person," dutifully conformed to societal norms and gender expectations. Often overlooked as a donor, she subscribed to the traditional roles of attentive wife, personal confidante, and civic volunteer. In her husband's frequent absences, Mary personified the adage: "They also serve who stand and wait." She maintained a comfortable home, knitted for the Red Cross, and sold war bonds with her close friend First Lady Edith Wilson. In a 1943 *Woman's Home Companion* interview, the magazine described her daily routine: "She reads and blue pencils books,

Mary G. Jones. From the Jones (Jesse Holman) Papers, CN Number 11342, courtesy Center for American History, U.T.—Austin.

clips the Houston papers her husband hasn't always time to read. She does all his shopping." In fact, the magazine added, the only thing she did not do was "to have his suits fitted on him!"[17]

According to biographer Timmons, "her greatest joys came from the charities they planned together." Mary not only enjoyed "helping people" but shaped the scope of their permanent philanthropy, the Houston Endowment, by focusing on traditional issues of female giving—education, children, health, and the arts. Having attended Methodist College in Waco, she was an avid reader who promoted higher academic standards for women, encouraging them to attend school by awarding college scholarships. Several buildings bear her name, in particular, the Mary Gibbs Jones College at Rice Institute, now Rice University, which provided a place for women to live on campus for the first time. She also aided children through foundation support of the Buckner Orphans Home, the National Kindergarten Association, and the Children's Lunch Fund. Furthermore, she was instrumental in underwriting the radio broadcast of the Houston Symphony and the Metropolitan Opera, thereby making classical music available to all Houston residents. As an opera patron and member of the Houston Foundation board of trustees (1954–62), Mary—along with John T. Jones, nephew and board president—was influential in the construction of the Jesse H. Jones Hall for the Performing Arts in Houston, posthumously named for the donor. As a result, her contributions as a philanthropic partner helped leverage support for causes she deemed important, thereby challenging, in part, the confines of her "separate sphere."[18]

In 1946, after fourteen years of national service, the Joneses left Washington, D.C., and returned to Houston. But Jesse Jones, who resumed active management of his business and philanthropic interests, encountered a vastly changed city. Feeling like "a modern day Rip Van Winkle" who had just awakened after a prolonged slumber, he sensed its expansive transformation. During his absence, Houston's population had multiplied from 292,352 in 1930 to approximately 500,000 by 1945—an increase of over seventy percent. At the same time, the metropolitan area had almost doubled from 456,570 to nearly 800,000 residents. A modern, diversified economy, fueled by wartime demands, had replaced the city's earlier dependence on railroads and the cotton trade. As the largest city in Texas with the third-busiest port in the nation, Houston was well on its way to preeminence in the Southwest. In turn, such an economic boom fostered residential and commercial construction, which translated into increased profits for the "Jones interests." The former New Dealer, now "a pacesetter in the postwar building boom," deftly enlarged his fortune again over the next several years. As a consequence, he was able to contribute an additional $2.7 million to the Houston Endowment, including his "entire salary" of $143,783.81 from government service.[19]

Yet another Houston also existed, one that Jones and the ruling business elite had partially neglected. With low taxes and paltry public services, the city faced serious infrastructure problems—flooding, sewage, pollution, and inadequate transportation. Equally important, pernicious segregation stratified the community, now a sprawling metropolis in the Jim Crow South. Black neighborhoods, concentrated in wards east of the downtown district, had received little attention from the city. They often did not have paved streets, running water, adequate drainage, or competent schools. Despite the 1954 *Brown* v. *Board of Education of Topeka* Supreme Court decision banning segregation in public-funded schools, conditions had not immediately improved. Uneven development, low-wage jobs, and racial separation persisted. Mexican Americans fared only slightly better. Resented for their willingness to work cheaply and their failure to learn English, they were often relegated to the most menial jobs the city had to offer. In short, the social costs of a good business climate, sociologist Joe R. Feagin observed, continued to be "disproportionately borne by the city's minority and low-income white residents."[20]

Jones, typical of philanthropists of this region and era, did not use his wealth and status to challenge the existing social relations. For instance, he and other Houston elites opposed the resurgence of the Ku Klux Klan in the 1920s primarily because of its violent tactics, which adversely affected business. While Jones's *Houston Chronicle* denounced the "invisible empire" and its message, it fell short of advocating racial integration. Like many other Southerners, Jones had acceded to the view that segregation did not constitute discrimination, so long as "separate but equal" facilities were provided. For example, at the 1928 Democratic National Convention he had permitted black spectators to attend the meeting but separated them from white delegates behind chicken wire. Similarly, his philanthropy reflected the existing race relations. Rather than racial equality, Jones used his resources to assist minority groups within the prevailing class system, favoring institutional solutions—not social reform. Jones therefore contributed financially to the United Negro College Fund and to black cancer patients at M. D. Anderson Hospital. He also donated heavily to the Beulah Baptist Church, as well as to historically black institutions such as Texas Southern University and Tuskegee Institute, the school founded by Booker T. Washington that put a premium on vocational over professional training. Like many other white philanthropists of his day, Jones believed that education through accommodation was the tonic that would provide minorities "equality of opportunity."[21]

After 1946, as Jones resumed a more "hands-on" philanthropic role, the consolidation of vast wealth in private foundations, such as the Houston Endowment, became increasingly controversial. Why? As the number of start-up foundations accelerated, fueled by the postwar prosperity and more favorable tax laws, confidence in philanthropic foundations as instruments for social good waned. Critics increasingly challenged the wisdom of granting tax-exempt status to organizations that diverted money from the public till, thereby reducing needed revenues. Others suspected that charitable concerns, rather than standard-bearers of public virtue, were merely vehicles to maintain dynastic control of family businesses. During the volatile cold war era, detractors questioned the power wielded by such elite, unelected, and often-secretive organizations, particularly their role in underwriting political action through international grants disguised as combating communism. Correspondingly, congressional interest rose as well, leaving philanthropic institutions vulnerable to legislative attack.[22]

By the decade of the 1950s congressional oversight of foundations began in earnest, posing potential problems for the Houston Endowment and other private foundations. Beginning with the Revenue Act of 1950, the government outlawed certain "prohibited transactions" by charitable groups and denied tax exemption on "unrelated business income." The law, which endeavored to correct fiscal abuses by donors and compel trustees to distribute their charitable funds, particularly targeted large, philanthropic organiza-

Jesse H. Jones and Dr. W. R. Banks. From the Jones (Jesse Holman) Papers, CN Number 11343, courtesy Center for American History, U.T.—Austin.

tions operating profit-making businesses such as the Houston Endowment. Accordingly, in 1951 the Internal Revenue Service sought to collect an additional $551,200 in taxes from the Houston Endowment, disallowing 1947–48 rent payments by the Commerce Company "either [as] an assignment of income to the exempt charitable corporation or the payment of a dividend in the guise of rent." Although the government ultimately failed to prove its case and collect back taxes, the attack placed private giving through foundations under a microscope and prophesied additional scrutiny. In the opinion of Houston Endowment attorney George A. Butler, this issue and other public concerns were "by no means settled for future years."[23]

Butler was right. In 1952 and again in 1954, the Cox and Reece congressional committees conducted hearings into alleged misconduct by educational and philanthropic foundations. Coinciding with the McCarthy-era "witch hunts," these probes assailed private grant-making organizations as "centers of subversion." In the course of the investigations, the Cox committee sent an eleven-page questionnaire to more than 1,500 private institutions, including the Houston Endowment. House members requested detailed information on grant-making policies, board composition, operating expenditures, and potential communist affiliation, all of which was provided. They also interrogated key witnesses. After months of painstaking testimony and internal controversy, the committees ultimately gave the Houston Endowment—and a majority of American foundations—a clean bill of health. Nonetheless, they issued several recommendations, ranging from full disclosure of financial data and a limit to foundation expenses to the elimination of improper donor influence and dismissal of trustees who approved grants to "subversive organizations." Although not supported by force of law, these proposals led to greater circumspection by the philanthropic community and forced the Houston Endowment to reexamine ways it had traditionally operated. The trustees recognized that, in the future, the accumulation of tax-exempt income, the assumption of long-term debt obligations, and the composition of its governing board would need to be carefully monitored.[24]

On June 1, 1956, the death of Jesse Jones from complications of "uremic poisoning" ushered in a new era for the Houston Endowment. Eighty-two-year-old Jones had left an estate structured to provide the fund with a solid basis for future success. He bequeathed to the foundation, which had received annual gifts during his lifetime, 5,000 shares of Commerce Company capital stock, valued at more than $3.4 million, as well as another $1.1 million from insurance policies. This bequest increased its assets from $31.9 million to $36.4 million. The remainder of his estimated $4.3 million estate, less cash gifts to relatives, friends, and employees, the executors held in trust "for the use and benefit" of his wife Mary. Jones directed in his will that, after her death, the residuary estate become the property of the Houston Endowment. He further stipulated that any assets that the foundation received would "be used within the State of Texas." This legal action, which altered the original trust agreement, insured that the foundation would not incur any onerous inheritance tax penalties on bequests used outside Texas. Changes simultaneously occurred in its grant-making policies as well. In 1958 the trustees inaugurated an additional educational program that provided four $2,000 scholarships for each graduating class in the Houston Independent School District. Henceforth, with its financial future secure and its academic outreach broadened, the Houston Endowment, following the death in 1962 of Mary Gibbs Jones, became the largest foundation with one of the fattest purses in the state.[25]

President Howard Creekmore, "the dean of foundation heads in Texas" for more than three decades, also left a distinctive mark on the Houston Endowment. Befriended by Jones as a young law student, Creekmore soon advanced within the Jones empire. Starting as a bookkeeper and then working as general counsel, he ultimately served on the board of trustees beginning in 1959. Five years later he became the endowment's president, responsible for managing its approximate $193 million in assets. Under his tenure Creekmore traded and sold various commercial properties in accordance with the Tax Reform Act of 1969 while increasing the endowment's value to more than $650 million. At the same time he directed the development of its grant program, guiding it from its brick and mortar phase to an emphasis on more "social and quality of life problems." All the while, Creekmore and the other trustees, all related to Jones by blood, marriage, or former business association, maintained strict control over the foundation. By keeping the board small, composed largely of self-perpetuating family members, Creekmore believed they could act promptly and re-duce the danger of financial malfeasance.[26]

The creation of the Houston Endowment in 1937 was largely a product of a man and his times. An astute businessman with a strong philanthropic impulse, Jesse Jones characteristically applied his sound, rational business methods, which had gen-erated great wealth and built an empire, to dispose of his discretionary income as well. He understood the potential of a grant-making foundation to promote favorite causes, particularly education, while providing benefits of tax reduction, donor con-trol, and a perpetual legacy. In short, this new form of philanthropy allowed Jones to pursue his vision of a just and equitable society, using his considerable talents within the prevailing socioeconomic culture of early-twentieth-century Texas.

By practicing large-scale "wholesale philanthropy," Jones also charted a course un-like most rich Texans of his day. Instead of maintaining a lavish lifestyle, sustaining traditional giving patterns, or accruing a sizable personal nest egg, he established a permanent vehicle for his giving—one structured on a corporate model and admin-istered during his lifetime. Furthermore, he was only one of a few Texans who cre-ated a charitable endowment during the Great Depression—a period when many fortunes were in ruins and New Deal programs supplanted private giving. While many naysayers were decrying the encroachment of big government and prophesy-ing the decline, even the destruction, of private philanthropy, Jones, drawing on his extensive public experience, understood the limitations of the federal bureaucracy. Rather than scaling back assistance, he contended that individual effort must con-tinue to supplement government programs. The unprecedented economic crisis af-ter 1929 did not signal the death throes of private initiative, as many believed, but instead fostered a mutual accommodation between the public and private sectors. Moreover, as a Southerner with strong communal ties, he also sought to preserve a measure of individualism and local control through the use of private funds for public purposes. Hence, during the third New Deal (1937–38), Jesse Jones created the Houston Endowment as a sound business investment but, more significantly, as an important counterweight to government expansion and as a permanent realiza-tion of his broad philanthropic goals.

F O U R

THE OTHER PRIVATE SPHERE
Miss Ima and the Hogg Foundation for Mental Health, 1940

I N AUSTIN, TEXAS, A TALL WEATHERED OBELISK dominates a tree-shaded plot in
the oldest section of Oakwood Cemetery. This monument, facing west toward the
state capitol, soars to twenty-five feet, dwarfing nearby memorials. Engraved on its
granite cornice is a bold letter "H" with a simple inscription of lineage etched in its
massive base. A three-foot ornamental hedge encloses the quiet sanctuary, conceal-
ing two stone benches and several unadorned grave markers. At the northwest corner towers a lone native pecan tree, symbolizing the dying wish of its deceased
benefactor to establish Texas as "a land of trees." Through this outer perimeter a narrow footpath opens onto a grassy enclave, past a trio of headstones, and toward the
imposing monolith. Only an unobtrusive seal of the Daughters of the Republic of
Texas suggests the import of the shrine. This serene setting, hushed and still, is the
final resting place of two generations of the Hogg family—Texas Governor James
Stephen Hogg, his wife, three sons, and daughter Ima.[1]

Like the striking memorial, family patriarch James S. Hogg cast a long shadow
across Texas, leaving a rich legacy of public service and private philanthropy. From
1891 to 1895 Hogg served as the first native-born governor of the state. During that
time he steadfastly championed the cause of the common man, supporting antitrust
legislation to curb the growth of monopolies and establishing a Railroad Commission to correct some of the worst industry abuses. The governor also used his
considerable political powers to advocate universal education and to expand the
University of Texas as the "capstone of our public free school system." Hogg, as a
private citizen and civic steward after 1895, devoted his retirement years to acquiring financial independence, improving schools, and promoting reform. On March 3,
1906, he died after a prolonged illness. He was, according to biographer Robert C.
Cotner, an outstanding executive, a forerunner of the Progressive movement, and
"one of the four great statesmen in Texas."[2]

The second generation of the Hogg family also demonstrated traits of public-
spiritedness, supporting numerous philanthropic and educational endeavors. Eldest
son Will, who managed the family's many oil investments and real estate ventures,
inherited a strong sense of civic duty. "The government," he observed, "made a mis-
take originally in not reserving for its own use all the wealth below the soil. What I
don't pay back in taxes on the oil which should not have been mine, I'm glad to give
away for the public welfare." A millionaire by age forty, he therefore forsook a re-

strictive business career for community service—what he called "bigger game abroad." Imbued with the ideals of his father, he dedicated his time and wealth to worthy projects, none more assiduously than to the University of Texas. In addition, Will generously aided numerous causes such as student loans for education, cash gifts to Texas colleges, land for recreational parks, and donations to youth organizations. Mike Hogg, the second son, paralleled the career of his father as well. He served from 1927 to 1930 in the Texas Legislature, in which he similarly defended the rights of the downtrodden against the encroachments of big business. Following his death in 1941, he bequeathed the residue of his estate to his wife, and then afterward to the University of Texas Board of Regents for a Department of Municipal Government at the university. Youngest son Tom, although little was known about him, also came to understand the moral responsibility of great wealth. Upon his death in 1949, he contributed the remainder of his property, after the life interest of his widow, to help fund the Hogg Foundation for Mental Health, a charitable trust established in 1940.[3]

The Hogg family legacy of civic stewardship did not end with these male descendants. Governor Hogg's daughter, affectionately known as "Miss Ima"—no other identification necessary—continued such philanthropic visions, eventually eclipsing her family's many achievements. Raised with a sharp sense of noblesse oblige, a concept that linked the duties of the rich to the society that had enriched them, she too regarded inherited wealth as a public trust. "I was taught that every citizen has an ob-

ligation to serve humanity according to his talents and privileges." Constrained both by law and custom within a separate "woman's sphere," she remained "invisible" for much of her early life; however, like Margaret Olivia Sage, "the foremost woman philanthropist of her age," Miss Ima gradually came to exercise public influence and private authority otherwise denied her. As the heir to the family fortune, she dutifully carried out the lessons absorbed in childhood and observed in adulthood: to defend "the cause of the common people," battle "for the weak against the strong," promote "free education for all," and, equally important, accomplish "whatever little good" possible.[4]

Ima Hogg, sometimes referred to by journalists as "the first lady of Texas," experienced a long, rich life, spanning

Ima Hogg, ca. 1940. From the Hogg (Ima) Papers, CN Number 11344, courtesy Center for American History, U.T.—Austin.

almost a century. Born on July 10, 1882, in Mineola, Texas, she enjoyed a privileged lifestyle. After spending much of her youth in Austin, first as the daughter of the governor and then later as a University of Texas student, she moved to New York in 1901 to study music. Following the death of her father, Miss Ima, a slender woman with "grace, skill, beauty," and exemplary character, sailed to Europe to pursue a career as a concert pianist. She eventually abandoned her performing ambitions, returning to the United States to teach piano and to continue her lifelong interest in the arts, including antiques, dance, literature, painting, decorative objects, and historic preservation. Exhibiting little interest in the flourishing family business—the Hogg Brothers, Inc. (a name that did not reflect her ownership)—Ima relied on her brothers to represent her interests. Devoted to the memory of her father, she never married but spent her days defending the former governor from his detractors. Imprinted with the nineteenth century "cult of true womanhood," which elevated women to guardians of home and hearth, she was entrusted with overseeing the construction of the Hogg family home, Bayou Bend, in the posh River Oaks section of Houston, as well as safeguarding the health and morals of her siblings. "Your influence over them," her father wrote to her in 1902, "is potent and far-reaching." Then, in her later years as she enlarged her sphere, Miss Ima assumed the role of an esteemed grande dame similar to that of Alice Roosevelt Longworth, daughter of President Theodore Roosevelt, in Washington, D.C.[5]

Despite her privileged status as the offspring of a populist governor, Ima, like all Texas women, encountered numerous legal disabilities, which restricted her full participation in the public sector. Not only was she denied the right to vote until 1920—disfranchised by the U.S. and Texas constitutions along with "idiots, lunatics, paupers," and felons—but also her ability to conduct business was severely limited. She could not serve on juries (until 1955), nor could she make contracts or write a will without a husband's signature. Moreover, when her brother Will died in 1930, leaving a sizable estate for some future "foundation or benefaction," as the next eldest she could not serve as executor; rather, Will designated her as counselor to younger brother Mike. Nevertheless, as a single woman she exercised more rights than a married woman, and, if she chose, could lawfully manage some of her own affairs.[6]

Like her brothers, Miss Ima inherited not only a sense of public duty but the funds to realize her own altruistic vision. She eventually profited handsomely from her father's purchase of a 4,100-acre tract of land—the old Varner plantation near West Columbia, Texas. Meanwhile, however, with the oil discovery at Spindletop on January 10, 1901, her father had acquired mineral rights to fifteen acres of land on the salt dome in Beaumont. He then joined with friend James Swayne of Fort Worth to form the Hogg-Swayne Syndicate, later merging with the Texas Company that would become better known as Texaco. Despite the drop in crude oil prices to three cents a barrel after the initial boom, Hogg continued to be optimistic about his West Columbia acreage—a field near the region of the Spindletop discovery. He had noticed oil seepage that would burst into flames when touched by a lighted match. As a consequence, on January 26, 1902, he wrote Ima an excited letter, forecasting that "prospects are good" and that he awaited "a gusher." She obtained further encouragement from her brother Will who predicted early in December, 1902, to "see 'em gush by Christmas," and then jubilantly declared: "Prepare to become a comfortably rich woman." She did. By the spring of 1903, the West Columbia land yielded fifty barrels a day, which they confidently believed "proved the field." Their optimism was premature. Not until after several more years of drilling did the first large well "blow in" with an initial flow of 100,000 barrels per year, later increasing to an astonishing two million barrels! As a result, by January of 1919 Ima Hogg witnessed the opening of a new, rich oil-bearing tract that would provide the seed money for realizing her philanthropic goals.[7]

Although James Hogg never survived to realize the enormous wealth from his West Columbia property, his descendants did—and prospered. By the terms of his will, he bequeathed to his four children "a modest estate" with an estimated worth of $138,000. He further stipulated that the Varner plantation, as yet an unproven oil field, remain within the family for "at least fifteen years," thus unknowingly securing their birthright. Hogg then allotted Ima two-thirds of its property value, with the remaining one-third given to Mike. Tom and Will divided the mineral rights. All, however, eventually shared in the gross income from the estate, totaling $225,000 a month after the oil discovery in 1919. Such profits, Will wrote his brother Tom, easily provided a "grub stake" for each sibling to attain financial independence, invest profitably, and live comfortably.[8]

With the death of Will Hogg on September 12, 1930, the disposal of his sizable estate created the corpus of the Hogg Foundation for Mental Health, administered by the University of Texas. Because he never married and had no descendants, Hogg intended that his approximately $2.5 million grant—the biggest in school history—should profit his alma mater. He also expressed the desire in his will, drafted March 7, 1928, to combine his funds with those of his sister Ima for some future endeavor that would bring "far-reaching benefit to the people of Texas." The final use of his gift—a reflection of his philanthropic spirit, as well as a desire to control his assets posthumously—remained ambiguous. Nevertheless, on July 15, 1939, after prolonged litigation and uncertainty, the University of Texas received the residue of his estate, valued at that time at approximately $1.8 million. Thus, Will Hogg had provided the seed money for a permanent fund that would establish "one of the largest and newest philanthropies" in the state.[9]

Due to the indefinite language of his will, however, the exact purpose of his bequest to Texas citizens remained obscure. How should the university use the funds? While a legal battle over inheritance and transfer taxes ensued, Mike Hogg considered several options for the money with "the good judgment and opinion" of his sister Ima—an acknowledgment of her moral authority. Among the potential recipients were three possibilities: a Brazoria county agricultural school for South

Texas boys, a lecture series on "history, literature, art and social and political experiences," and a trust fund "for the common good of all or any part of Texas." After considerable deliberation, Miss Ima recalled in 1961, Mike forthrightly stated: "Sis, why don't we decide to leave the principal part of the estate to the University for mental health?" Because her brother was "the first one to put it into those words," she immediately agreed. "That is just exactly the right thing," she responded, as this was a cause she had long championed. Moreover, a chance meeting with University of Texas President Homer P. Rainey on May 5, 1939, as they traveled to the McDonald Observatory dedication, confirmed the school's interest, thereby solidifying her resolve. Anxious that "her brother's estate be put to a cause of such potential benefit to human welfare," Ima Hogg then announced "a broad mental health program" as the recipient of support. She envisioned a statewide program that would be both "preventive and therapeutic," as well as provide educational information to rural and urban areas throughout the state. This determination, Miss Ima believed, amply fulfilled her "Brother Will's aspirations and intentions." In 1940, at age fifty-eight, she pioneered a hybrid philanthropic entity—the Hogg Foundation for Mental Health—that was both an operating and grant-making organization affiliated with a public institution.[10]

Initially, the Hogg heirs excluded the family name from their foundation title but later acquiesced. Both executor Mike and sister Ima neither cared for nor sought publicity in their giving. In fact, a full accounting of Hogg benefactions did not exist. They desired anonymity so that others would support this philanthropy and "not feel that they were giving to a special family." Close associates nevertheless convinced them that name recognition served as powerful testimony to the moral responsibilities of great wealth, as well as a dual inducement for others to support their cause. Mike and Ima therefore added "Hogg" to the foundation name—in honor of their parents.[11]

By 1940, however, Ima Hogg had reached a turning point in her life. With the death of Will and Mike's two-year bout with cancer and subsequent demise, she necessarily assumed control of the Hogg estate, acquiring new responsibility, increased self-confidence, and personal independence. Like many Texas women, Miss Ima had been recognized more for her volunteer services such as organizing fund-raisers and attending charitable balls. She had already assumed leadership positions in many wide-ranging projects that had garnered her a modicum of recognition, including the Houston Child Guidance Center, the Houston Symphony, and the Houston Community Chest. By the early 1940s she expanded her role. Now a middle-aged matron, she employed public service and private philanthropy as her access to the wider world. She challenged the confines of her "separate sphere," a position both privileged and subordinate, by serving her first and only term of elected public office (1943–49) on the Houston Board of Education—elected at the age of sixty-one. Most importantly, Miss Ima pioneered the creation of the Hogg Foundation for Mental Health.[12]

The selection of mental health as the mission of the Hogg Foundation generated

considerable speculation and conjecture. Some suggested that the concept had originated from the emotional and mental anguish of Texans during the depression of
the 1930s. Unemployment, homelessness, and hunger had eroded the human spirit,
contributing to instability, insanity, and even suicide. A mental health program, with
an emphasis on education and prevention, might mitigate social conditions and
bring useful information to "every day people." Others cited Miss Ima's enduring interest in mental illness—its causes and cures. As a child she had traveled with her father, whose approach to behavioral problems was "far ahead of his time." She had
accompanied him to numerous hospitals and prisons where she observed inmates in
need of "better mental health." Moreover, as a University of Texas coed she had developed a "principal interest" in psychology—a relatively new discipline—studying
with A. Caswell Ellis, a leading authority in the field and lifelong friend. Still others
theorized that her own severe bouts of depression and insomnia, particularly after
the deaths of her parents, as well as the emotional afflictions of younger brother Tom,
prompted her to support the cause. Whatever the reason, Ima Hogg vowed to do
something positive about the problem when time and resources permitted.[13]

Heretofore, organized philanthropy was essentially a male preserve. Few elite
white women established private foundations or gained credit for their use of private
capital to leverage important social change. But as women in Texas and elsewhere
gained control over their estates, a few such as Ima Hogg established permanent organizations as repositories for their surplus wealth. They recognized, like their male
counterparts, the need for a more systematic approach to the allocation of their charitable dollars, as well as the responsibility of using unexpected wealth wisely. Thus,
whether through marriage, career, or inheritance, women helped shape their communities, using female wealth for the public good.

From its inception, Miss Ima played a vital and innovative role in the Hogg Foundation. She grasped the concept of mental health, commonly referred to as mental
hygiene at that time, and understood, far in advance of her contemporaries, the
importance of prevention. By identifying this complex and often-concealed social
problem, she brought her unique talents to bear upon finding a solution. According
to her brother's wishes, she also purposefully restricted grant recipients to Texas residents, thereby exempting the fund from burdensome inheritance taxes. "I believe
every state should take care of its own," she cogently asserted. "The nearer home you
come, the better you can operate." Equally important, Ima Hogg established a foundation at a time when few of her sex either held public office or exercised financial
power apart from their spouses. While many progressive women bridged the gulf between public and private spheres through "organized womanhood," such as voluntary associations, church guilds, and women's clubs, Ima seldom joined such groups;
instead, she preferred individual action. By conceiving, guiding, and helping fund
the Hogg Foundation, Miss Ima assumed a rare autonomy, acquiring important
public skills and a degree of power at a time when socially constructed roles for the
sexes prevailed.[14]

Ima Hogg, while fashioning an alternative sphere through foundation philanthropy, however, did not seriously challenge the status quo. As a typical "lady bountiful," she maintained both the class system and culture from which her privileged position arose. Nurtured by a society that placed southern women on a pedestal, she never joined the suffrage or women's rights movements of the era or significantly contributed to their causes, although she was surely aware of their goals. This elite female model, according to cultural anthropologist Teresa Odendahl, was typical, observing that it was "difficult for wealthy women to be feminists, for they are contesting a system that privileges them in other regards." Neither was she a radical for progressive reforms; instead she preferred "reasoned logic" to push independently for favorite causes, many of which perpetuated traditional patterns of female giving—social work, women's education, and child welfare—as well as conventional standards of male governance. As Hogg Foundation secretary and personal friend Maud Keeling recalled: "Miss Ima was not a 'feminist'—but a 'humanist.'"[15]

Nevertheless, Miss Ima wielded financial resources as powerful tools for social change. Her mental health advocacy helped create new career opportunities for women in nursing, counseling, and teaching. Her championing of children's charities aided mothers and restored families. Meanwhile, the work of the foundation supported women's shelters and funded studies for those abused and neglected. Later, in 1965, the establishment of a separate Ima Hogg fund from her private resources greatly expanded mental health services among the children of Houston.[16]

For the remainder of her life Miss Ima placed primary importance on the creation and direction of the Hogg Foundation. Ascribing to the philosophy of oil tycoon and philanthropist John D. Rockefeller Sr. that the person who controlled the money should also be personally involved in the giving, she never wavered from her commitment. "My first obligation," she reminisced in 1967 at age eighty-five, "is to this Foundation." A year later, Ima reiterated: "My interest in mental health is as strong as ever." As a consequence, she continually exerted "good judgment and opinion"—qualities her brother Will had earlier valued—to help set its agenda and guide its course.

From the determination of its mission statement to the appointment of its first director, sociology professor Robert Lee Sutherland, Ima Hogg served as a strategic donor rather than a meddling type. She consistently provided "intelligent inspiration of a broad nature" that transformed the foundation from a privately controlled institution to a public trust governed by grant-making professionals. Rather than trusted family members or close associates, she relied on experts in the mental health field, thereby providing public accountability decades before other foundations adopted such practices. In turn, Sutherland and his staff often sought her advice, kept her informed, and encouraged her participation. They especially valued "the daring and breadth of [her] ideas," which were uniquely ahead of the times. As a consequence of her direction, the Hogg Foundation became the first professionally organized foundation in Texas—another hallmark of modern philanthropy.[17]

Ima Hogg and Dr. Robert Sutherland. Courtesy the Hogg Foundation for Mental Health.

As a student of the human condition, Ima Hogg held firm beliefs concerning the implementation of a mental health program. She based her ideas on the philosophies of psychologists Austin Riggs and Will Menninger. They advocated that all persons should seek their purpose in life—one in which they believed and could dedicate their energies. Yet, no one was perfectly balanced and at some time or another "everyone needs help." As a consequence, Miss Ima stressed the importance of prevention rather than the treatment of mental illness. Such intervention, she maintained, "must start at the roots," that is, at the early stages of life. She subscribed to Margaret Sage's dictum that "the only remedy for the social evil in any Anglo-Saxon country is apparently in the education of children—boys and girls." Accordingly, Ima Hogg recommended that foundation grants be channeled toward "practical matters for action" aimed at the young. "I think we already know more than we put into practice," she recalled in 1961, "and this is where I think the emphasis should be placed." Preventive mental health education and child guidance programs, rather than new research, she believed, were more likely to curb juvenile delinquency and restore families.[18]

After years of preparation, the trustees, director, and staff of the Hogg Foundation officially inaugurated its mental health mission on the Austin campus. In a three-day conference, February 11–13, 1941, U.T. President Rainey formally installed Sutherland, a man with "a broad social science background of training and experience." Many outstanding speakers shared the forum, addressing a wide range of issues from "Who Now is the Educated Person?" to "The Personal Equation in Modern Living." The organizers also sought to demonstrate the application of mental hygiene "to all phases of community life," ranging from university students and social workers to law officials and religious leaders. Conference leaders specifically wanted to publicize the two-fold purpose of the new foundation: "to set up a state-wide program of mental hygiene and to carry education throughout the state by means of endowed lectureships."[19]

With a director, a part-time assistant, and an operating budget of $20,000, the Hogg Foundation, housed in a small University Tower office, focused initially on mental health education. This decision permitted the trustees to carry out immediately the foundation's mandate to "benefit the people of Texas" by providing valuable information on the subject. Consultants, referred to as "circuit riders," traveled the state, visiting small towns and rural areas to hand out booklets on family life and problem solving. T. V. Smith, a university professor and politician, initiated this statewide tour, speaking on the importance of "Education During a Crisis." During the first year, these lecturers reached approximately 135,000 persons through more than 656 public sessions, increasing to 184,500 by 1943. Foundation staffers also mailed participants additional publications that promoted their program and built a small readership. As a result, thirty-three Hogg Foundation monographs reached approximately 2,000 subscribers, representing all regions of the state.[20]

During the first decade of its existence (1940–50), the Hogg Foundation enlarged its outreach. Working during World War II with the Texas State Selective Service Board, the staff developed screening methods "to prevent the maladjusted from entering military service." So effective were such procedures that other states adopted the Hogg pattern. At the same time, they also counseled wartime casualties such as "shell shock" victims, as well as assisted displaced workers on the home front. In addition, consultants held workshops and training sessions for newly recruited counselors and volunteers in the Red Cross and United Services Organization. When travel and funding were curtailed due to military priorities, the Hogg Foundation adapted, turning to "Lectures in Print" to carry its message to the public. With the end of hostilities in August, 1945, foundation programs evolved to aid more than 600,000 returning veterans and their families adjust to peacetime living. The foundation also placed increased importance on public schools, assigning visiting teachers, or "psychiatric social workers," to individual campuses and encouraging short mental health courses at the university level. In 1948, in response to growing postwar demands for additional social services from the private sector—exacerbated by returning soldiers and increased urbanization—Sutherland helped organize the Conference of Southwest Foundations. This new "community of foundation leaders," the first in the nation, would meet yearly to "share experiences and information" with similar groups to maximize philanthropic efforts throughout the state and region.[21]

During the early postwar era (1950–60), the Hogg Foundation continued to develop, adopting a pluralistic approach to mental health. Taking into account all potential components that influence human behavior—family, community, career, school, and government—Director Sutherland defined the foundation's mission broadly and adopted a willingness to experiment. While maintaining the mental health emphasis, he expanded services by funding research projects and establishing partnerships with community programs. The staff trained professional workers, aided mental health clinics, and strengthened ties to the academic departments of the University of Texas. The board of regents also formed a national advisory council in 1959 to provide expert guidance and later a medical advisory council to ensure objectivity regarding the "great diversity of requests for funds." Much of these new activities, as well as the hiring of Wayne Holtzman as the new director of research, were made possible through the additional financial support from Hogg family members, including Miss Ima, Alice Hogg Hanszen, and the estates of Mike and Tom Hogg.[22]

In the 1960s the Hogg Foundation expanded its mission to meet the larger problems of society. While work with other Texas foundations continued, it established a regional funding library under the auspices of the Foundation Library Center of New York to aid grant seekers in obtaining funding. The foundation also targeted special populations such as ethnic minorities and the aged for mental health services. In 1963 the Hogg Foundation received a $550,000 five-year grant from the Ford Foundation to conduct a new program, "Philanthropy in the Southwest," which would offer a "wealth of experience in project-funding" to administrators of Texas funds. As a result, requests for aid poured in, ranging from budget design to staff reorganization. Then, on August 1, 1966, the mass shooting from the observation deck of the Austin University Tower, where staff members watched in horror, underscored the need for expanded mental health services. Renewed efforts by the foundation led to the establishment of the U.T. Counseling Center with crisis services available to students on campus.[23]

During the decade of the 1960s several new philanthropic funds helped enlarge the resources of the Hogg Foundation. In 1964 Ima Hogg approved the articles of incorporation and bylaws for a trust bearing her name at the University of Texas. Terms of Miss Ima's will of January 5, 1965, earmarked "all real and personal property," not specifically bequeathed, to benefit the Ima Hogg Foundation and to be activated upon her death. She stipulated that the income from her sizable estate should promote mental health among the children in the Houston area, especially the Child Guidance Center, the Children's Mental Health Services, and the Hope Center for Youth, Inc. She also directed the university trustees to allocate $200,000 to the Houston Symphony for a permanent endowment; however, if the Symphony Society ceased operation for three consecutive years, all gifts reverted to the Hogg Foundation. Following her death on August 19, 1975, from a coronary occlusion at age ninety-three, the foundation was able to provide additional grants to worthy projects benefiting the children of Houston and Harris County.[24]

By 1970 the Hogg Foundation, widely recognized as a pioneer in the field of foundation philanthropy, had earned a national reputation as "the foundations' foundation." This epithet arose from its groundbreaking efforts in the field of mental health, its interaction with statewide agencies and organizations, and its collaboration with other charitable groups in the region. The willingness of its executive officers to experiment, seeking imaginative solutions to everyday problems earned respect and recognition from the philanthropic community. For instance, during Sutherland's tenure, the foundation enacted innovations such as the acceptance of supplemental gifts, the formation of joint partnerships, and the utilization of matching grants. Furthermore, the Hogg Foundation was one of the earliest Texas funds to apply objective criteria to its grant-making, rather than relying on personal recommendations and trustee referrals. These strategies soon established the foundation as a leader in the field and a resource to other potential donors for consultation and assistance. Fittingly, the 1951 annual report of the Carnegie Corporation praised the Hogg Foundation in laudatory terms for "doing a vigorous and constructive job," as well as providing "leadership in effecting an exchange of information and ideas among all foundations."[25]

During its first three decades (1940–70), the Hogg Foundation for Mental Health grew in size, delivering a broad mental health program "of great benefit to the people of Texas." With a meager budget in 1940 of $20,000 and a limited staff, by 1970 the foundation had increased its operating funds to more than $547,000 a year, with two active advisory committees, numerous consultants, three executive assistants, and thirteen full- and part-time employees. Such expansion also necessitated new office space, requiring the Hogg Foundation to move from the twenty-fourth floor in the University Tower to the Will C. Hogg Building on the University of Texas campus. Then, with the retirement of Robert Sutherland after thirty years, a new director, psychologist Wayne Holtzman, and a second generation of professionals assumed leadership, signaling the end of an era that was noted for its "strong-willed donor and a soft-spoken, effective director."[26]

The long-lasting nature of the Hogg Foundation for Mental Health attested to the spirit, determination, and vision of Ima Hogg. As a benefactress of great wealth, she used her financial resources both to enlarge her private sphere and leverage important social change in Texas. In an era when mental illness and its manifestations were little understood or openly discussed, Miss Ima utilized her private wealth for the public good through education, prevention, and detection. At the same time, she demonstrated the values that women bring to philanthropy, as well as the opportunities available to them in the public sphere. Although neither a crusader for the women's movement nor a typical "southern lady" confined to the home, Miss Ima charted an independent course. By fusing the admonition of suffragette Susan B. Anthony "to have a purse of her own," with the counsel of Margaret Olivia Sage "to find a beneficent outlet" for her wealth, Ima Hogg challenged the bonds of womanhood. She not only provided an avenue of meaningful work for herself, but also significantly improved Texas society through the creation of the Hogg Foundation for Mental Health.[27]

FIVE

BRAGGIN' RIGHTS
Amon G. Carter, Community Identity, and
Cultural Philanthropy, 1945

"NO OTHER INDIVIDUAL AND NO OTHER CITY in the United States [is] so inextricably identified with each other as Amon Carter and Fort Worth," syndicated columnist Inez Robb wrote in 1949. As publisher of the *Fort Worth Star-Telegram* and owner of radio station WBAP, Carter whole-heartedly embraced the city "Where the West Begins" that had contributed to his remarkable success. Believing that "a man can not live off his community, but must live with it," he devoted his life work to "making the world conscious of Fort Worth," while promoting his own interests and that region of irregular plains, limited rainfall, and sparse population known as the West. Carter, at times derisively criticized for his boastful swagger and theatrical antics, was an indefatigable civic booster who claimed "braggin' rights" for his adopted city. As a tireless promoter and self-proclaimed "menace to Dallas," he often exaggerated, sometimes chastised, but always encouraged his fellow townsmen to greater effort. Energized by his consummate vision and forceful personality, Fort Worth citizens united behind his leadership, subscribing to his daily newspaper and supporting a diverse array of Carter-sponsored municipal projects and economic ventures. This mutual relationship, born out of the realization that his business prospects were closely tied to those of the community, helped transform Fort Worth from a small, frontier outpost in 1849 to a growing metropolis of "cows, culture, chivalry, stockyards, industry, and aviation" by 1950.[1]

Throughout his life Amon Carter exuded a certain restless energy and enterprising spirit typical of many Americans at the turn of the century. Born in an unchinked log cabin in Crafton, Texas, on December 11, 1879, he attended school until the age of eleven, necessarily dropping out after his mother Josie's death to earn a living working numerous odd jobs. In typical Horatio Alger fashion and with a strong dose of "pluck and luck," Carter moved to Bowie in 1890, a small town sixty-five miles north of Fort Worth. Despite his hardscrabble surroundings, he doggedly pursued various money-making ventures. From 1898 to 1905 the ambitious, self-reliant young man—almost six feet tall, of medium build, black eyes, dark brown hair, and with a prominent nose—traveled throughout the United States as a representative for a Chicago portrait firm and a San Francisco advertising agency. In 1905, aware of the burgeoning Fort Worth population and the arrival of the Swift and Armour meat packing and processing plants, Carter, then twenty-five years old, decided to relocate to "the city" of his boyhood dreams.[2]

For Carter, no place in the world held a greater attraction than Fort Worth. Located near the confluence of the Clear and West Forks of the Trinity River, the town, inhabited by "not more than three hundred souls" in 1870, acquired the Texas and Pacific Railroad and established a railhead and passenger hub for West Texas in 1876. Freight wagons and stagecoach lines provided regular service between the new depot and the hinterland. With its transportation needs met, the population of Fort Worth surged from 6,663 in 1880 to 26,688 by the end of the century—a 300 percent increase. In turn, economic prospects expanded; social activities multiplied; and the community acquired many of the trap-

Amon Carter. From the *Fort Worth Star-Telegram* Collection, no. AR 406-2-19-12B, courtesy U.T.—Arlington.

pings of a modern city—electric lights, street cars, macadamized roads, daily mail service, municipal water, a sewer system, and a central fire station. Cultural pursuits such as opera and music flourished as well, while recreational and educational facilities improved. Gradually, churches, libraries, and schools replaced saloons, bawdy houses, and dance halls. By 1885, despite its reputation as a "wide open boomtown," frequented by thirsty Chisholm Trail cowboys and rowdy patrons of Hell's Half Acre—a red-light district known for its violence and lawlessness—the roughness of frontier life was fading. Journalist B. B. Paddock cogently observed in 1887: "The city prospered. Everybody prospered, and life in Fort Worth commenced to adorn itself with comforts and delicacies."[3]

Ironically, Carter, the foremost spokesperson of Texas ethos, arrived in Fort Worth after the frontier, with its wide expanse of unsettled lands and open range, had vanished. In 1893 historian Frederick Jackson Turner had dramatically announced the closing of this "great historic movement" in his classic but sometimes-besieged thesis, "The Significance of the Frontier in American History." By 1890, Turner argued, Americans had established their hegemony over the land, eliminating all other claimants, destroying the buffalo herds, and fencing off prime pastureland. As a consequence, farms, ranches, and cities gradually stretched out across the previously barren Texas landscape. A definable frontier had vanished from the American landscape. Although Carter was born too late to have participated in full measure in nineteenth-century expansionism, the settlement of the West—especially the Anglo occupation of Texas with its "horse and gun" culture—left an indelible imprint that would influence both his "getting and giving." Justly proud of Fort Worth's history, its traditions, and its seemingly unlimited prospects, Carter became convinced that his chosen hometown, often hailed as the "Queen City of the Prairie," offered the best opportunity to escape from the dreary mesquite and scrub-oak plains of North Texas, end his vagabond ways, and begin his life's work.[4]

In 1905 Carter capitalized on his intuitive salesmanship skills and formed the Texas Advertising and Manufacturing Company of Fort Worth, whose principal products were a patented indexing telephone directory and promotional streetcar cards. A year later, while attending a demonstration of a new energy source—buffalo chips saturated with crude oil—he encountered two ambitious entrepreneurs, newspaper reporters D.C. McCaleb and A. G. Dawson, who were scouting for financial investors. With little money but considerable persuasive powers, he convinced them to hire him as advertising manager for a new business venture—the *Fort Worth Star,* an afternoon daily to rival the *Fort Worth Telegram*. Soon thereafter, Carter deftly negotiated the merger of the two papers and by 1923 became president and publisher of the *Fort Worth Star-Telegram*. Two years later he consolidated his journalist empire with the purchase of the *Record* from interloper William Randolph Hearst. For the next thirty-two years, the "one-man Chamber of Commerce" and "political giant" remained a powerful force in Fort Worth, helping shape its economic growth, community identity, and cultural development.[5]

As a successful businessman who personified the Jeffersonian ideal of "careers open to talent," Carter was an ambitious and generous man—both for himself and his community. Popular accounts of his activities typically emphasized his diverse roles as a civic booster, picturesque showman, and lavish entertainer; he was the quintessential public relations man who peddled newspaper advertisements, entertained the masses, and "sold" Fort Worth. Carter simultaneously proved to be an unselfish philanthropist. Inheriting from his mother a strong sense of regard for those less fortunate, Carter engaged in numerous private acts of charity—what biographer Jerry Flemmons called "fits of philanthropy." Beginning with his *Star-Telegram* employees, he paternalistically provided them with liberal benefits, Christmas bonuses, and emergency assistance at a time when "he was making very little more money than the men in the composing room." He also remembered the corner news carriers by giving each a silver dollar at annual Thanksgiving dinners, which at that time was a sizable sum, and awarded Amon G. Carter Jr. scholarships to paperboys with the highest high school grades. "Money, to him," retired *Star-Telegram* printer Dave Keith recalled, "was more of something to lift others up with than to hoard for himself."[6]

Carter used the considerable power of his newspaper to identify with the people of West Texas and their problems. He wanted the *Star-Telegram* to be their voice, their advocate and protector, especially in regard to the poor and the downtrodden. During the hot summer months Carter sponsored a free milk and ice fund for the needy, and, during the Christmas season, he provided toys and candy through the Goodfellows Fund for disadvantaged children. Moreover, media stories about personal misfortune or distress elicited an immediate response of aid from the publisher. For instance, Carter paid the hospital bills of a family critically injured at a railroad crossing, as well as the expenses for several medical operations for a youth hurt in a motorcycle accident. He was also an indefatigable fund-raiser, directing capital campaigns to construct a Young Men's Christian Association and vigorously supporting numerous charitable causes such as the Mississippi Flood Relief (1927) and the Damon Runyon Cancer Fund. Carter, although deprived of formal schooling, championed higher education as well. In 1923 he supported the establishment of a four-year college in Lubbock and in 1930 personally contributed to the efforts to erect a football stadium at Texas Christian University. Little wonder then that his name was the first inscribed in the Book of Golden Deeds by the Exchange Club, an exclusive Fort Worth men's organization.[7]

Yet such "hands-on philanthropy," which characterized Carter's individual and future large-scale giving, did not address the deep-seated racial and social problems of early-twentieth-century Texas. Like Jesse Jones and other philanthropists of this era, Carter aided minority groups within the prevailing class system of racial segregation. For example, he gave $25,000 to improve Como Park, a recreational area for black residents, $200 to support a segregated YMCA, and $500 to assist a black membership sorority. He also provided educational opportunities for African Americans, usually at segregated colleges such as Prairie View A&M. Such gifts, according to a local paper, were "proof of Mr. Carter's interest in the colored citizens of Fort Worth." But concern did not encompass reform; and his philanthropic efforts, although praiseworthy, did not challenge the status quo governing social relations in Fort Worth.[8]

Initially, Carter funded many of his public interests and charitable gifts through the *Star-Telegram;* but with escalating debts and mounting loans, he necessarily sought supplemental sources of income to continue his largess. In 1920, with the fabulous West Texas and Panhandle oil discoveries, he tried "wildcatting" and "struck oil," later selling his investments for $100,000 to pay off a number of obligations. Years passed, however, without another gusher, and Carter became known as "the only big producer who never produced." Then, in 1935 after ninety dry holes, he at last struck oil again at the Mattix Pool in New Mexico. Two years later he drilled the discovery well in the vast Wasson Pool in Gaines and Yoakum Counties—"one of the largest in the state, second only to East Texas production." This bonanza, along with the 1926 oil depletion allowance that allowed producers a liberal tax deduction, alleviated his financial worries and thereby provided the seed money for his philanthropy.[9]

Thereafter, according to broadcast journalist Mrs. Edgar Deen, his "giving seemed endless." For instance, he provided for a wide variety of needs—air conditioning for polio patients at John Peter Smith Hospital, carillon bells for the Culver Military

Academy in Indiana, a lighting system for Amon Carter Riverside High School, and a summer camp for local Boy Scouts. But, most importantly, the oil revenue formed the nucleus for the establishment of a more permanent vehicle for his philanthropy—the Amon G. Carter Foundation. Founded in 1945 at the conclusion of World War II, this new private fund would usher in a new era of organized giving.[10]

A self-made millionaire at age fifty-eight, Carter not only dispensed innumerable, often unpublicized, gifts of varying sizes but practiced large-scale philanthropy as well. On April 7, 1945, along with former wife Nenetta, he created the Amon G. Carter Foundation to support "benevolent, charitable, educational or missionary undertakings." Widely recognizable with his signature Shady Oaks felt hat, cream-colored polo coat, and blue-brown cowboy boots, Carter served as its first president, continuing his "hands-on philosophy" of giving; Nenetta, however, having moved to New York in 1941 following their divorce, did not play an active role. Son Amon Jr., daughter Ruth, longtime secretary Katrine Deakins, Presbyterian minister James Thompson, and local physician Webb Walker completed the first governing roster, serving unpaid, staggered terms. The *Star-Telegram* housed the foundation offices, thereby simplifying its grant-making operations and reducing overhead costs. On June 23 the state chartered the organization as a general-purpose, nonprofit foundation. This status, like the Houston Endowment and others, limited the financial liability of its officers and assured its standing as a tax-exempt institution. Thus, at age sixty-five, Carter joined the ranks of the more than ninety other Texas philanthropists and their families in creating a permanent fund to support causes, assist institutions, and promote values that he deemed important.[11]

Why did Carter turn to large-scale, organized philanthropy after more than thirty years of individual giving? Was it simple altruism, estate planning, or a hope of remembrance? As in the case of most human affairs, his motives were mixed. Affection for his community and a desire to enhance its respectability surely contributed to his decision. Believing that West Texas suffered from a lack of recognition, he had consistently channeled his energy and wealth into permanent institutions for the region, such as airports, schools, and hospitals, as a tangible expression of that sentiment. For example, when an advisory board of historians to the 1936 Centennial Commission rejected the city as its site on the grounds that West Texas "contains no history to commemorate," he single-handedly financed and held a rival exposition! In the process, he built the Will Rogers Memorial Coliseum and municipal auditorium, which became the capstone of his promotional efforts and integral parts of the early Fort Worth skyline. Such cultural monuments, according to foundation scholar Waldemar Nielsen, helped fill the need for a "social infrastructure," which the region—and the city—so desperately lacked. Carter continued this successful formula of promoting and building Fort Worth—and at times denigrating Dallas, its closest competitor—by establishing a lasting vehicle for his philanthropy, namely the Carter Foundation, and then largely restricting its grants to Texas, especially Fort Worth and Tarrant County.[12]

Organized philanthropy also represented a sound business decision for Carter. As daughter Ruth emphatically stated, the immense fortune he derived from successful oil exploits allowed him to realize his own altruistic vision, but it incurred enormous tax liability. Increases in the federal tax codes during and after World War II necessitated financial planning lest the government appropriate the bulk of his large estate. Additionally, by later structuring a "Texas only" clause in his will, Carter could avoid state inheritance taxes. With family members and trusted associates sitting on the Carter board of trustees, dynastic control over company funds could be maintained, thereby perpetuating economic and cultural influence. Thus, after 1945, private foundations became "the order of the day" for astute businessmen and women with great personal and corporate wealth. Although altruism and devotion to Fort Worth surely influenced the creation of the Carter Foundation, the financial benefits accrued by such action also permitted Carter to protect his assets, reduce his liabilities, and practice philanthropy on a princely scale.[13]

Several other factors may have indirectly led Carter to set up a philanthropic foundation. Like many other wealthy Texas donors, Carter subscribed to the notion of civic stewardship as outlined by Carnegie in "Wealth." Carter wrote in his will: "I have come to realize that they who acquire wealth are more or less stewards in the application of that wealth to the human family who are less fortunate than themselves." What better way, then, to continue his vision of stewardship than to seek a more permanent form of philanthropy by establishing a private foundation? Then again, after amassing his vast fortune, personal appeals for assistance may have overwhelmed him. Industrialist John D. Rockefeller at times received more than fifty thousand "begging letters" a month; likewise, Carter and secretary Deakins complained that such petitions "bogged down" their office, perhaps necessitating a more institutionalized framework for his giving. With the end of World War II and the long-awaited return of son Amon Jr., a prisoner of war incarcerated in Poland, perhaps Carter wanted to devote full measure to his financial and charitable endeavors. Or maybe like other mortals, Carter may have yearned to secure his final legacy, thereby silencing his critics, increasing his status, and perpetuating his name after death. Whatever the reasons, and without totally abandoning charitable "handouts," he embarked on a course of institutional philanthropy in 1945 with the same zeal and determination that he brought to advancing his career, supporting worthwhile causes, and "selling" Fort Worth.[14]

In similar fashion to Jesse Jones and the Houston Endowment, Carter initially set a time limit for the completion of his institutional giving. The "Rule Against Perpetuities," established by the Texas Constitution of 1876, prohibited "many types of interests in property" to continue indefinitely. In the twentieth century, this provision included tax-exempt foundations created by living donors. As such they were considered to be monopolies and contrary to "the genius of a free government." Whether Carter shared this aversion to perpetual endowments, like Sears heir Julius Rosenwald, who wrote that "philanthropic enterprises should come to an end with the close of the philanthropist's life, or, at most, a single generation after his death," or simply followed the letter of the law, remained unclear. Nevertheless, Carter designed his foundation to expire after fifty years, providing for the expenditure of both its capital and income, if necessary, much as Rosenwald recommended. At the end of the allotted time all remaining money and property not required to fulfill existing obligations or commitments would become the property of Texas Christian University in Fort Worth.[15]

Chartered in 1945, the Carter Foundation began active operation in September of 1947. With proceeds from the sale of the Wasson Pool holdings to the Shell Oil Company for $16.5 million, Amon and Nenetta Carter funded the endowment, sixty and forty percent, respectively, with more than $8.5 million. During its first five years, grants totaled more than $1.5 million, thereby benefiting a number of schools, churches, and youth groups. One early award provided funds to purchase the William Luther Lewis literary collection of rare first editions and original manuscripts of important English and American authors, housed at TCU. Then, on June 23, 1955, after Carter died at age seventy-five from a preexisting heart condition, the foundation acquired the balance of his $10.2 million estate, less part interest in Carter Publications, Inc., as well as money and property previously allotted. As residual legatee, the foundation thereby boosted its endowment another $7.2 million and enlarged its mission to meet the expanded terms of Carter's will.[16]

The manner in which individuals have left their money after death has often revealed how they wanted to be remembered. Carter was no exception. Beginning with his final resting place, he directed in his will that his executors erect "a suitable mausoleum," attesting to "the love I held for my fellow-man and my devotion to the cause of the weak and the underprivileged." The crypt, built on a western slope in Greenwood Memorial Cemetery in Fort Worth, bore a simple inscription: "His Life Made Charity as Real as Hope Itself." He further articulated definite ideas concerning the institutional distribution of his wealth. Unlike the foundation articles of incorporation that stipulated broad philanthropic goals, his final testament specified the "burdens, obligations and payments" assumed by the endowment. For example, Carter directed the trustees to earmark annual payments of $24,000 to third wife Minnie Meacham Carter, to award $50,000 over ten years for scholarships to Amon G. Carter Riverside High School students; and to allocate $100 per annum to a Christmas Tree Fund at the Fort Worth Lodge of the Benevolent and Protective Order of Elks. He also purposefully limited the geographical scope of his benevolence to recipients exclusively "within the State of Texas," thereby avoiding estate taxes on gifts outside the state.[17]

Carter, attuned to the demands of the new global era—oil, aviation, and automobiles—also felt a strong obligation to his local roots. Community mattered to Carter, and he wanted to return a portion of his wealth to his hometown and region. "I am a part of the heritage of Texas," Carter wrote. "I wish to share it with others who would make Texas their home and their inspiration." Then, in keeping with his devotion to Fort Worth, he bequeathed his extensive art collection—"paintings of great value," statuary, sculpture, and other objets d'art—to the foundation. No longer content with the exclusive enjoyment of his works, Carter enjoined the officers to establish a museum to house the Amon Carter Collection of Western Art. He specifically wanted to "aid in the promotion of a cultural spirit." Hence, he further directed that the foundation operate the facility, at least until the city had sufficient funds to assume its management. At that time the Carter Foundation would deed the building and its contents to the community. Thus, by specifying permanent beneficiaries such as an art museum and committing funds to its support, Carter protected his legacy from the sort of "hit-and-run philanthropy" characteristic of other private grant-making institutions.[18]

For Carter the practice of cultural philanthropy was an extension of his personal philosophy. Denied formal schooling as a youth, he came to define "educational" in broad terms, including not only institutional learning, but "interest in and knowledge of paintings, sculpture and other things of an artistic nature." Besides, daughter Ruth later recalled, he was always in too much of a hurry for "the lengthy perusal of books and manuscripts or for the hearing of music." He therefore eschewed intellectual pursuits and rarely attended theater, dance, or opera. Instead, Carter fancied the visual arts because of their "immediacy." In the 1920s he began collecting "scenes of the West or themes relating to the life of that region," many times borrowing the money for his purchases. To Carter the pioneering spirit depicted on such canvasses and bronzes, which included an impressive group of works by artists Charles Russell and Frederic Remington, symbolized a heroic, bygone era distinguished by values of honesty, fortitude, hope, tenacity, and stick-to-itiveness. With a sense of nostalgia, if not regret, at the passing of these frontier traditions, Carter, through a museum devoted to western art, sought to legitimize and transmit this heritage to future generations "without payment or fee or charge whatsoever."[19]

Carter further reasoned that the presence of an art museum might shore up the sagging image of Fort Worth as an unrefined cowtown, a perception fostered by his advertising slogan: "Go to Dallas for education [and culture]; Come to Fort Worth for entertainment." By cultivating its aesthetic spirit, engaging its youth in "artistic imagination," and restoring its competitive edge with rival Dallas, which already touted an active cultural community, the museum would bring to the city national recognition and make art a regular part of urban life. Cultural philanthropy, then, was an instrument Carter used to come to terms with the hopes and fears that he held for his city. At the same time a Museum of Western Art was good business sense. Such an institution not only celebrated the uniqueness of the region, thereby infusing Fort Worth with a distinctive "personality," but it also helped lure new businesses and attract wealthy patrons who might otherwise have located elsewhere.[20]

Although Carter envisioned such a permanent Fort Worth gallery during the early 1940s, the Museum of Western Art was a posthumous creation. The pleasure of daily living with his numerous art works—around his office, at the Fort Worth

Club, and in his home—precluded their removal to a public venue until after his death in 1955. Moreover, financial problems entangled the foundation for a number of years and then difficulties finding "the right architect" for the museum postponed the project. But by 1959, with legal obstacles resolved and the addition of an adjoining tract of city land, trustee Ruth Carter Johnson (later Stevenson) guided the undertaking to completion, occasionally referring to the project as her "sixth child." On January 24, 1961, the new museum opened its doors to a large crowd, despite an icy winter storm. "It shows that the world is not as immune to culture as we are led to believe," Ruth Johnson commented. Located on "a noble slope overlooking the city's center," the building, fashioned by New York architect Philip Johnson from native Texas shell stone, faced "the rising sun like the Plains Indian lodges." Described by foundation president Amon G. Carter Jr. as one of his "dad's fondest dreams," it displayed more than two hundred Russell and Remington paintings, as well as pen-and-ink drawings and illustrated letters. Considerable memorabilia, fourteen Remington sculptures, and more than sixty Russell bronzes, comprising the only complete collection in existence of original castings, rounded out the impressive collection. C. R. Smith, president of American Airlines and a member of the five-man museum advisory committee, placed the opening day in perspective: "This museum and these paintings are held for a specific reason and purpose, because Amon G.

Museum of Western Art, Fort Worth. From the *Fort Worth Star-Telegram* Collection, no. 4734, no. 16, courtesy U.T.—Arlington.

Carter loved the days of the pioneer and he wanted to give you an opportunity to form an affection for these sturdy men and women of the earlier days."[21]

Yet the Carter Foundation, despite its pioneering cultural and charitable mission, was not immune to the growing climate of mistrust and skepticism enveloping organized philanthropy in the "third sector." As the number of private foundations increased in the United States during the 1940s, neither donor motives nor their decisions were beyond question. The Carter Foundation, with a high-profile founder and large purse, did not escape scrutiny. For instance, in 1957 the federal government examined Carter Foundation tax payments. Citing the Revenue Act of 1950 that permitted taxation of "charitable and other tax-exempt foundations on 'unrelated business income,'" the Internal Revenue Service imposed assessments against the Carter Foundation of approximately $1.6 million, including interest. Asserting that the IRS had erroneously collected the money, the Carter trust officers filed suit in federal district court on May 9, maintaining that the Carter Foundation Production Company, the target of the IRS probe, was a separate corporation that merely "owned and operated oil properties once held by the foundation." Moreover, they argued that the company had previously paid taxes on its income, and the foundation had received "nothing from the properties" that would fall within the IRS definition. By January, 1958, the court agreed. Six months later, on July 18, the government dropped the case from the Fifth Circuit Court of Appeals.[22]

Four years later, however, Representative Wright Patman of Texarkana conducted another inquiry into private foundations and their "undesirable concentration of economic power." His concerns were real and seemingly legitimate. He alleged that 534 tax-exempt groups, including the Carter Foundation, failed to comply with federal tax codes. Patman specifically charged that they had neglected to inform the IRS of stock ownership in private business corporations. Although Texas foundations were never the nerve center of Patman's ire—he was targeting larger, national ones instead—he placed the Carter Foundation, along with eight other Texas funds with assets of "no less than $10 billion in 1960," on a list of suspect institutions. A yearlong investigation ensued. During that time an IRS agent was assigned to the foundation office and "had to be provided with a desk, typewriter, and other materials," according to Ruth Carter Stevenson. The agent examined financial records, questioning board grant-making policies, especially those proposals that were denied. Stevenson, a board member at the time, charged that the investigation was "politically motivated," citing the fact that the *Star-Telegram* "did not support Lyndon B. Johnson," a Democrat, as the reason for the audit.[23]

Confronted with a different political climate, the Carter Foundation, with its tax-exempt status and self-perpetuating board of directors, came under fire—for understandable reasons. Specifically, it had never issued an annual report; it held stock in business activities that distracted from its philanthropic responsibilities; and it provided little public accountability—all potential abuses that deserved correction.

Patman characterized such large grant-making organizations as "financial ogres" and unleashed an eight-year investigation into American foundations, which posed the most serious challenge to organized giving. "Philanthropy, one of mankind's nobler instincts," Patman declared, "has been perverted into a vehicle for institutionalized, deliberate evasion of fiscal and moral responsibility to the nation." While his probe uncovered no specific evidence of wrongdoing by the Carter Foundation, the acrimonious hearings, nonetheless, uncovered financial abuses and irregularities by other organizations. Because "no odor [is] so bad as that which arises from goodness tainted," as writer Henry David Thoreau observed in 1854, Congress drafted legislation to address concerns about the place of private foundations in a democratic society.[24]

The protracted Patman investigation resulted in the passage of the Tax Reform Act of 1969, with its landmark regulatory provisions. The law, written with the aid of Representative Wilbur Mills of Arkansas, enacted six major reforms: a four percent annual excise tax on net investment income, prohibitions against self-dealing, a six percent annual pay out of assets (later lowered to five percent), a twenty percent limitation on ownership of any corporation, restrictions on political activities, and various disclosure requirements. These new conditions were far less draconian than many had feared, but they fundamentally altered the character of organized philanthropy. Future privately funded, tax-exempt foundations, guided by the values of their donors, would also have to exist as public trusts; not only should they fulfill their philanthropic missions, but foundations would have to become more transparent, remaining open and accountable to society at large.[25]

Despite the mercurial and sometimes adversarial public-private relationship during the early cold war era (1945–70), the Carter Foundation received two major infusions of capital—the initial endowment from oil proceeds in 1947 and then additional revenue from the Carter estate in 1955. The demise of its donor in 1955 significantly redefined its mission, narrowing the scope to Texas and earmarking approximately twenty-five percent of its resources (later increased to fifty percent) to fund an art museum. A second generation also assumed leadership: son Amon Jr., who replaced his father as board president in 1947; Ruth Carter; and Katrine Deakins, who continued on the board of directors. Then, in 1960 Texas Secretary of State Zollie Steakley certified the first amendments to the foundation's articles of incorporation, thereby nullifying its fifty-year life span, imposing a "perpetual existence," and reducing the number of directors to three. These changes effectively removed TCU as the final legatee of the Carter fortune and restricted grant-making decisions to a few close family members. Furthermore, with the passage of the Tax Reform Act of 1969, the federal government pressured tax-exempt organizations to dispose of their profit-making businesses. In response, the Carter Foundation began plans to divest itself of its holdings, eventually selling radio station WBAP and the *Star-Telegram* to Capital Cities Broadcasting Corporation, a New York media giant, for $80 million, and WBAP-TV to LIN Broadcasting Corporation, also of New York, for $35 million.[26]

At the same time, Carter Foundation grant-making policies matured, gradually shifting from funding brick and mortar projects to sponsoring more social programs and human services. For example, wider outreach into the community supported the needs of women and children, health care, crime prevention, animal rights, and the elderly. As a result, by 1970 the foundation had evolved from a private, general-purpose philanthropic institution—with an active donor and little professional staff—to one of the ten-largest, permanently endowed foundations in the state, charged with the task of promoting the "cultural spirit" and general welfare of Texans.[27]

By the time of his death in 1955, Amon G. Carter had pioneered large-scale philanthropy in Fort Worth. As a civic steward and "purveyor of culture," he had influenced the character of an entire city and region. Furthermore, his early efforts had inspired other wealthy Texans to widen their philanthropic horizons and establish charitable funds as well; hence, the Bass Foundation (1945), the Sid Richardson Foundation (1947), and the Burnett-Tandy Foundation (1968) organized. Similar to the Carter Foundation, they too maintained a "hometown" focus with oil revenues providing most of the seed money. As a result, Fort Worth enjoyed "more foundation funds per capita than any other community in the country," Mayor Bob Bolen observed. Carter's leadership and largess were instrumental in the development of a cultural district in the city. In the decades that followed, Fort Worth acquired the Kimbell Art Museum, the Botanic Garden Conservatory, the Water Gardens, and, most recently, the Bass Performance Hall. By establishing the Carter Foundation as a permanent vehicle for his philanthropy, Carter served not only Fort Worth and West Texas but himself, protecting his investments while promoting his own distinctive vision of community and culture. As Houston philanthropist and builder Jesse Jones fittingly wrote in 1946: "Fort Worth would not be Fort Worth without Amon Carter."[28]

S I X

BUILDING A PHILANTHROPIC COMMUNITY
The Conference of Southwest Foundations, 1948

F ROM 1920 TO 1950 TEXAS LED THE SOUTHWEST in the creation of philanthropic
foundations. The state lagged behind other regions nationally but by mid-
century boasted nearly 180 such grant-making organizations. (See Table 1.) Although most had arisen from small-to-mid-size family fortunes as independent
endowments, community, corporate, and operating funds appeared as well. Philanthropic forecasters predicted that Texas' robust economy and expanding population
of 7,711,194 by 1950 would spur an "Age of Foundations" to rival New York and
other industrial eastern states in organized, charitable giving.[1]

Despite such phenomenal growth that mirrored national trends, early Texas
foundations operated in isolation. As the first generation of funders, trustees had
little experience or knowledge of the philanthropic world outside the original intent
and guidance of their donors. Boards were usually composed of legal heirs or close
advisors who had meager access to skilled staffs or adequate understanding of societal needs. Moreover, many remained unaware of similar charitable work performed
by corresponding organizations throughout the state. "We know nothing about
them, and they know nothing about us," recalled Maud Keeling, secretary of the
Texas Foundations and Trust Funds, now the Conference of Southwest Foundations. In addition, few books or publications offered practical instruction in grant
making or foundation management. And no statewide directory of chartered foundations existed. As a result, duplication and division prevailed in the allocation of resources by Texas foundations.[2]

Such conditions changed. In the fall of 1948 three foundation representatives met
"by sheer chance" near the University Tower building in Austin. Members of this
serendipitous group included Robert Sutherland, director of the Hogg Foundation
for Mental Health (1940), Mary Elizabeth Holdsworth Butt of the H. E. Butt Foundation (1933) in Corpus Christi, and Margaret C. Scarbrough of the Lemuel
Scarbrough Foundation (1944) in Austin. While conversing over lunch, the trio
shared their mutual interests in philanthropy as well as their concerns: How could
small family foundations secure information? What could they accomplish without
a staff? Did other charitable organizations face a similar plight? At the same time,
they also discovered that each had approved identical grants for post-graduate education at the University of Texas. Such a revelation aroused their interest in other
statewide foundations and their benefactions, as well as fostered a desire for better

communication, greater efficiency, and continued contact.[3]

Initially recruited by Sutherland to help organize the philanthropic community, Mary Butt and Margaret Scarbrough proved equal to the task. Both women were already civic volunteers in their communities, assisting the poor, building libraries, supporting mental health programs, and providing chest X rays to Hispanic residents. In fact, Mary Butt, a member of a devout Baptist tithing family, was an unusual social activist of that day, particularly as an advocate for the health and educational needs of South Texas families. In addition, both had earlier joined their husbands in establishing Texas foundations. The Lemuel Scarbrough Foundation funded local religious and educational projects from its flourishing Austin department store income, while the H. E. Butt Foundation sup-

Dr. Robert Sutherland, Mary Elizabeth Butt, and Margaret Scarbrough. Courtesy the Conference of Southwest Foundations.

ported public libraries and recreational facilities from its successful grocery store profits. As grocer Howard E. Butt Sr. once stated: "I make the money, and Mary spends it [on worthy causes]. And I'm glad she does."[4]

In the spring of 1949 CSF pioneers Butt, Scarbrough, and Sutherland organized and later hosted the first Conference of Texas Foundations and Trust Funds, although no name existed at the time. Unaware that they were "founding anything," but simply responding to a need, Sutherland extended informal invitations to approximately fifteen foundations, mostly family endowments with which the three were personally acquainted. In an introductory letter he explained that the purpose of the proposed "get-together" was to exchange ideas about programs and procedures in the administration of philanthropic funds. This "exploratory conference," he later pledged, was not to pool resources but to discuss the operation of trusts, trends in philanthropy, and the needs of the Southwest.[5]

On March 31, 1949, with assurances that the forum would not become "an organization of fund seekers," representatives from ten Texas foundations assembled at the Driskill Hotel in Austin for what turned out to be a historic one-day meeting. The participants, along with consultants from the General Education Board of the Rockefeller Foundation, the Carnegie Foundation, the Community Chest of San Antonio, the Southern Education Foundation, and the University of Texas, exchanged brief accounts of their missions and chronicled the charitable activities of their organizations. A luncheon discussion followed, featuring tax recommendations—an increasingly important issue—from William B. Bates of the M. D. Anderson Foundation, as well as grant-making comments from U.T. President T. S. Painter and U.T. Board of Regents Chairman Dudley K. Woodward. An "afternoon analysis" completed the schedule, with a question-and-answer session chaired by Fred McCuistion of the Rockefeller General Education Board, brief remarks from U.T. Dean H. L. Haskew, and preliminary observations from Director Lester Swander of the San Antonio Community Chest. As the meeting concluded, all agreed that this initial round table had proven invaluable. Mary Butt, described as "a woman bubbling with ideas," pronounced the proceedings "a delightful and profitable day," while Margaret Scarbrough, with her characteristic "vivacious and energetic" style, portrayed the events as a "fairy story sequence of words." The attendees then enthusiastically elected Sutherland as interim chairman and unanimously voted to meet again. With this final action the delegates adjourned, thereby unofficially designating this family gathering of Texas philanthropists as an annual reunion.[6]

Central to the success of these early conferences was the Hogg Foundation for Mental Health. As a mid-size philanthropic institution with a small paid professional staff, this organization assumed the primary financial and operational responsibility of the fledgling group. Director Sutherland, a widely respected sociologist and an engaging lecturer, volunteered Hogg offices for its administrative needs, while his assistant, Maud Keeling, oversaw the day-to-day tasks. Initially, she considered such additional work as "a little extra chore," but gradually Keeling and the Hogg Foundation staff assumed increasing duties—planning the yearly meetings as well as typing, printing, and mailing conference materials. Because membership fees were nonexistent at the time, the Hogg Foundation also paid Keeling an hourly salary and travel expenses—sometimes totaling in excess of $1,300 a year. By 1954 the Hogg Foundation tower address, Main Building 2608, began to appear on conference letterheads—another outward sign of its sponsorship.[7]

As a charter member and unflagging supporter, Robert Sutherland epitomized, more than any other individual, the spirit of cooperation within the newly formed philanthropic community. Tall and lanky, with a relaxed demeanor, this renowned professor welcomed the opportunity to ensure that charitable funds were distributed in "the wisest way possible." In touring the state, Sutherland championed private philanthropy as a force in solving social problems and promoted an enlarged awareness of the needs of the Southwest. He drew on his considerable personal and professional skills—selflessness, sincerity, and an interest in the human condition—thereby applying his talents to recruit publicity-shy donors who feared becoming victims of unsolicited fund seekers. Ever resourceful and well-connected, he also arranged for business leaders and out-of-state consultants to attend conference meetings, most notably F. Emerson Andrews of the Foundation Library Center in New York. Sutherland further served terms as Conference of Southwest Foundations president and vice president, as well as chairman of numerous committees. His personality permeated the organization, inspiring frequent laudatory descriptions of him as a "mover and shaker," a man "generous of spirit," and "the real source of the dream."[8]

If Sutherland was the visionary, then the centerpiece of the organization was Maud Keeling. A petite women with dark brown, curly hair and a ready smile, she had studied sociology and psychology at the University of Texas before accepting a position with the Hogg Foundation in 1945. As secretary, researcher, and assistant to Sutherland, Keeling performed various duties before leaving for Europe in 1948 to study German. As a result, she missed the inaugural CSF meeting in March, 1949, but returned in the fall as a field representative to plan, organize, and execute the annual conferences. Without a staff or budget, Keeling single-handedly attended to CSF business—stuffing envelopes, designing covers, assembling programs, researching locations, and visiting host members. Although family responsibilities and job relocations (many out of state) intervened, she continued to coordinate the conference by simply taking the job with her. She recalled, "I kept one foot in the state of Texas. I would dictate a letter to a secretary in Dallas, my printer would be in San Antonio, and the Conference was being held in Oklahoma." The board of directors designated her home or business address—rather than that of the changing officers—as its headquarters. Keeling also faithfully attended every fall board and program committee meeting and the spring annual conference—a total of forty-six consecutive annual sessions! She also scrupulously catalogued CSF papers to provide an accurate and complete history of the organization. The summer, 1981, issue of the CSF newsletter "Cooperation" fittingly concluded: "To know her is to know the story of the Conference."[9]

From its earliest inception the CSF was a loosely defined group, composed primarily of donors from grant-making institutions in Texas—and then the Southwest. Its purpose was informal, described as an "exchange of ideas" to enhance the fulfillment of the charitable missions of its members. As a de facto organization, it operated without benefit of a constitution or bylaws, a budget or a name. Even its existence remained uncertain until 1952 when the delegates approved annual conferences and elected a slate of officers the following year. Yet this semblance of organization only reinforced the need for stricter guidelines: "We [still] did not know if we would continue," Maud Keeling stated. Particularly urgent was the ambiguous nature of membership qualifications. In addition to the legitimate foundations, representatives from diverse groups—persons eager to establish a foundation, receiving organizations hopeful of securing funds, as well as institutions dependent on private money—attended the meetings. Moreover, trustees from neighboring states participated, because CSF organizers jokingly suggested that any state in the National Collegiate Athletic Association's Southwest Conference was an automatic member. As a consequence, the CSF community and its boundaries remained fluid.[10]

The CSF gradually transformed itself from a neophyte gathering of Texas donors to a legitimate, nationally recognized leader in the field of foundation philanthropy.

1956 Conference of Southwest Foundation annual meeting. Courtesy the Conference of
Southwest Foundations.

During an eight-year period, 1948–56, attendance increased from ten to forty-eight
organizations and from twenty to more than one hundred participants, representing
a gain of approximately 400 percent! Grant-making behemoths such as the Houston
Endowment, with vast assets and professional staffs, mingled with the smaller, fam-
ily-run charter members. National publications, specifically *Business Week,* produced
articles about the conference, observing that Texas was "the only state that has an organization of people with money to give away, who meet to see where it should go."
Inquiries from out-of-state groups doubled, and requests for CSF consultants increased. A name change also reflected its expanding influence—from the Texas
Foundations and Trust Funds to the Conference of Southwest Foundations. Such
growing pains, however, necessitated an instrument for legal governance; hence, the
executive committee approved a constitution and bylaws in 1955 that were ratified
by the membership the following year. On December 9, 1957, Mary Butt prepared
a formal mission statement, which declared CSF intention "to stimulate individual
foundation thinking," and to promote "the same kind of practical forethought, energy and good common sense displayed by those who amassed the fortunes." The
board of directors elaborated on her idea and adopted the Statement of Aims and
Purposes; the membership unanimously approved it the following year. Thus, by
1958 the CSF had acquired all the requisites of a bona fide organization, with a
"minimum of machinery" to stage its annual meetings.[11]

As membership soared, so did appeals for elected leaders and additional services, which were readily met. At the fifth annual assembly in 1953 the CSF selected, albeit ex officio, its first slate of officers. Delegates chose Tom Slick of the Southwest Research Foundation in San Antonio as president and Bob Sutherland as vice president. At the same time, the organizers recognized the paucity of information available to current donors and prospective benefactors; therefore, they published a series of "occasional papers"—keynote addresses from the annual meetings—as well as reprints of articles on philanthropic trends. Responding to requests from smaller family trusts, the Lemuel Scarbrough Foundation sponsored the publication of three pamphlets: "What is a Foundation?"; "To What Can I Give?"; and "Tax Advantages of Foundation Giving." In turn, the Hogg Foundation established a lending library and circulated a list of available books and annual reports, and the CSF printed and distributed a preliminary directory of Texas foundations (1954)—the first of its kind. Then in 1955 the board of directors approved the creation of a "Clearing House of Foundation Activity," providing public access to sample charters, free consultants, and potential projects. Thus, if an individual wanted to set up a charitable fund, Keeling explained, "he could write to us and say he would like some help." Equally important, Southern Methodist University law professor and counsel to the Southwestern Legal Foundation John Riehm began attending conference meetings. He dispensed much-needed tax advice and provided legislative updates to the members as part of their estate planning. By 1957 the CSF produced its first quarterly newsletter, later named "Cooperation," to inform the expanding philanthropic community about relevant books, current activities, and future plans.[12]

The annual conference program also evolved to meet the needs of the Southwest. In the early years, the "get-together" consisted of trustee narrations of foundation projects and group discussions of common problems. By the fifth year, 1953, however, a printed program with guest speakers appeared and a new format for the general sessions emerged: an address of general interest, a speech or panel concerning philanthropic opportunities, and a presentation about current legislation and legal issues. The CSF frequently included a session on "How to Create a Foundation"—a nuts-and-bolts talk to prospective donors. Gradually, as the members became better acquainted, the conference expanded to a two-day meeting in which experts in fields such as medicine and education chaired informational workshops. In 1959 the annual conference moved out of state for the first time to Santa Fe, New Mexico—signifying its regional status.[13]

If change and progress characterized the growing community of philanthropists, so did stability and continuity. From 1949 until her retirement in 1996, Maud Keeling provided uninterrupted service as CSF executive secretary-director for forty-seven years. "She knew us all," Margaret Scarbrough cogently observed; indeed, she was "the heart of our progress, the rubric marker of the Conference of Southwest Foundations." With such remarkable dedication, Keeling and the charter members also adhered to the original intent of the founders. Eschewing the temptation to pool funds or solicit money for pet projects, they strictly preserved the informal forum based on the sharing of ideas and information. Conference officials, while recognizing the contributions from eleemosynary and grant-seeking institutions, purposefully maintained a relaxed environment limited to donor foundations. CSF member Andy Edington, a trustee of the Peterson Foundation in Kerrville, valued the casual gathering that allowed him and others to have "a good time" without driving members away with "a tight organization." Cooper Foundation director Jerry Cartwright of Waco observed that foundations were "a lonely business," but the CSF brought similar-minded people together to fulfill their charitable missions. This atmosphere of cooperation and community, what Bob J. Crow of the Amon G. Carter Foundation called "a philosophical fraternity," was the "one thing that has not changed and we hope it never will."[14]

But pressing financial concerns continued to afflict the growing organization. At its sixth annual meeting (1954) in Austin, several members proposed that the CSF adopt a self-supporting budget. For example, in the absence of membership or registration fees, the CSF could only request voluntary contributions, which totaled a mere $550 in 1954—an insufficient amount to sustain the organization. As a result, the fiscal burden fell on the Hogg Foundation and conference hosts. Although this arrangement had been "quite all right" with Sutherland and his staff, some representatives feared that the U.T. Board of Regents—trustees of the Hogg Foundation—might eventually question the propriety of a mental health fund subsidizing a meeting of Texas foundations. The next year the conference began collecting a four-dollar registration fee and established annual dues of ten dollars—curiously meager amounts for such wealthy donors. Nevertheless, this action enabled the organization to pay some of its debts and assume all of its office and travel expenses, as well as one-third of the salary of the executive secretary, thereby allowing the Hogg Foundation to reduce its generous support.[15]

Even more problematic than its financial health was the question of membership. While the conference operated without a constitution or bylaws for seven years (1949–55), it was primarily an informal gathering of small-to-mid-size grant-making foundations. Indeed, the membership shunned fund seekers for fear of "predatory supplicants." Nonie Thompson, a CSF past president, explained: "A long-standing tradition, a gentlemen's agreement, says that taking unfair advantage of one's members for soliciting purposes is not acceptable." Occasional abuses occurred. Such "begging incidents" convinced the founders of the necessity to formulate a precise member definition. At the seventh annual meeting in 1955 the CSF constitution and bylaws restricted its membership to "all bona fide tax exempt Foundations and Trusts . . . which have actively associated themselves with the Conference" prior to April, 1955. New members—limited to donor foundations and bank trust departments that administered fiduciary funds—joined through election at an annual or special meeting. At the same time, the territory of the Southwest—Texas, Arkansas, Oklahoma, Arizona, and New Mexico—became firmly established, not by legal means but by default as other areas of the nation claimed their areas and formed their own regional associations.[16]

The CSF membership, due to the economic and social conditions of early-twentieth-century Texas, was notably homogeneous in makeup. Foundation philanthropy, a product of Gilded Age prosperity and Texas oil wealth, remained the province of white, Anglo-Saxon, Protestant, male donors and trustees. The builders of these fortunes were mostly men who later sought rational, systematic methods to dispose of their colossal wealth. Few women, constrained by law and custom, had amassed large holdings or controlled sufficient assets apart from their husbands to establish grant-making organizations. Consequently, of the twenty persons present at the 1949 organizational meeting, only three females—Mary Butt, Margaret Scarbrough, and Ima Hogg—actively participated. All, however, had derived their resources through their roles as wives or daughters. At later conferences women continued to be underrepresented, with those female attendees performing mainly supporting roles as spouses or volunteers. Even more conspicuously absent were minorities such as Hispanics and blacks. At that time, low wages, few opportunities, and inadequate education consigned most to positions of recipients rather than grant makers. In addition, alternative patterns of giving, as well as discrimination, segregation, and poverty, precluded CSF participation by many potential "donors of color." Rather than utilizing institutional tools such as foundations and endowments, Mexican Americans traditionally donated funds in more informal ways to churches, individuals, and mutual aid societies known as *mutualistas.* African Americans, legally separated from mainstream institutions since 1896, also adopted a more personal approach; they supported local religious groups and created black self-help organizations. Furthermore, unlike "scientific philanthropy" that generally applied long-term solutions to social problems, minority assistance tended to address immediate needs of specific communities. Early CSF membership, like the vast majority of Texas foundations, reflected the political and social realities of the age, remaining the domain of affluent, white, male philanthropists.[17]

The CSF, a product of this period, also organized at a time when foundations and their benefactors were under renewed public scrutiny. Initially, critics had attacked grant-making institutions from the left, charging in 1915 that they were dominated by big business and supported conservative, even reactionary, causes. Such Progressive era opposition represented old Populist antagonisms toward special interests. But no regulatory action transpired. Not until almost four decades later, within the volatile cold war atmosphere, did detractors from the radical right, cloaked in anti-communist rhetoric, assail private philanthropy once again—this time as "centers of subversion." As the Cox (1952) and Reece (1954) congressional investigations probed the accusations, which alleged Moscow-directed plots to penetrate American foundations, witnesses from the private sector credibly defended their policies. In the process, "nearly all aspects of foundation operations" were disclosed. Such revelations exposed the shadowy world of institutional philanthropy and further emphasized its growing influence and power. Once again only mild recommendations resulted, thus effectively delaying any real reform until the passage of the Tax Reform Act of 1969. As historian Robert Bremner observed, these McCarthy-inspired investigative committees "did no serious harm to foundations."[18]

Nevertheless, the legislative hearings—at times angry and hostile—alarmed a segment of the Texas philanthropic community. Some CSF members resented public disclosure of what they considered private giving practices, believing that they "should neither seek nor attract notice." A few trustees feared outside interference into their grant-making decisions and governing policies. Others, worried about their vulnerability to future restrictive laws, threatened to become more circumspect and less open. As Maud Keeling succinctly stated: "They clammed up tighter than ever." Yet, despite some grave concerns that antifoundation publicity might someday destroy the independence of private foundations—one of the hallmarks of private philanthropy—most considered the House probes as remote, unfounded investigations and were "simply unconcerned by them."[19]

The public attacks, nonetheless, clearly exposed the frailties of foundation giving. As an elite, unelected, and often-mysterious group, donors and trustees exercised enormous power outside the democratic process. Many operated discreetly, shunning public controversy while pursuing private interests that tended to support elite institutions. Utilizing unregulated, tax-exempt funds—many established in perpetuity—they influenced a broad spectrum of public issues from education and research to art and recreation. Occasionally, governing boards diverted their charitable assets for political purposes, propaganda dissemination, or even legislative influence—charges later substantiated against the Hobby Foundation of Houston and others. Through their grant-making powers they further functioned as "purveyors of culture," according to sociologist Donald Fisher, exercising ideological and intellectual hegemony through their support or rejection of grant proposals. Without mandatory financial reports, many of these funding decisions occurred behind a shroud of secrecy. In short, as important power centers of American life, foundation scholar Waldemar Nielsen astutely observed, philanthropic organizations "were not controlled by market forces, electoral constituencies, bodies of members, or even formally established canons of conduct." Thus, by 1953, their public standing had diminished, foreshadowing future regulatory legislation of the 1960s and clouding the future of the CSF.[20]

Concerned about the intensifying opposition, as well as the lack of accurate information about foundations, CSF leadership recommended cooperation and candor to its membership—a practice already established by some of the larger eastern foundations. Philanthropic institutions, they asserted, could no longer afford to be perceived as clandestine operations. The CSF therefore advised that member organizations, due to their tax-exempt status, maintain "a wholesome front" by opening their records, issuing annual reports, and providing public accountability. Moreover, Sutherland consistently cautioned that private funds be used "for their intended purposes," specifically "non-political, scientific and humanitarian objectives." As public resentment increased through the 1950s, conference leaders continued to recommend a policy of openness and accessibility, urging members to eliminate obvious abuses and "to put their houses in order."[21]

Despite the negative publicity and popular skepticism, the number and assets of Texas foundations dramatically expanded during the post–World War II years, altering the makeup of the CSF. With a 300 percent increase in start-ups, peace, prosperity, and tax considerations contributed to the predicted "Age of Foundations." Second- and third-generation trustees replaced the early pioneers at conference meetings. More representatives from small foundations mixed freely with the staffs of larger organizations. Soon, concern with donor problems shifted to foundation responsibilities, particularly in providing philanthropic capital to new areas of service. Advice on "Ways Technology Can Assist Philanthropy" supplanted earlier how-to publications. As diverse groups increasingly acquired wealth and status, CSF membership became more inclusive, thereby initiating a broader range of charitable giving.[22]

From 1948 to 1970, the Conference of Southwest Foundations served as an informal, "learning, socializing experience" where a select group of donors interacted and exchanged ideas. The CSF, as the first cooperative community of philanthropists in the nation, pioneered a more efficient and informed allocation of surplus funds. Through its annual conferences it identified social problems, offered organizational support, and promoted foundation philanthropy as a vehicle to serve the people of Texas and the Southwest. Furthermore, its gatherings provided opportunities for collaboration, education, and fellowship. The CSF, by virtue of its elite membership, naturally tended both to reflect and maintain the social and economic order. With few women and no minorities, it promoted the cultural arrangements that gave rise to philanthropy in the first place. Organized during the early cold war, a period of intense public scrutiny, a few CSF members occasionally mismanaged private, tax-exempt funds, contributing to the traumatic encounter with Congress and the passage of the Tax Reform Act of 1969. Nevertheless, the Conference of Southwest Foundations represented a unique and powerful force for organized, charitable giving in the Southwest. As such, the CSF helped guide and define the Texas philanthropic experience.[23]

CONCLUSION
For the People of Texas

URING THE FIRST TWO DECADES of the twentieth century profound changes engulfed the nation. Rapid industrialization and technological improvements from the previous thirty years transformed the United States from an agricultural nation of small farmers to a modern society with global responsibilities. Such expansion, both swift and unregulated, produced an unequal distribution of wealth with a large capital concentration in the hands of a new millionaire class. At the same time, immigration and migration, spurred by the expanding economy, altered the American landscape, leading to a decline in rural areas and the rise of large cities. Social tensions, moral crusades, and military mobilization stimulated further changes in the home and the workplace. Given the escalating and largely unplanned nature of urban growth, overcrowded neighborhoods and sprawling communities soon outstripped municipal services. The problems of a modern society became more vexing, increasing demands on private charities, civic organizations, and eleemosynary institutions.

After the turn of the century, a philanthropic revolution occurred to meet the needs of a changing population. The influence of Carnegie's seminal essay, "Wealth," which emphasized enlightened giving, and the Progressive reassessment, which urged reforms at all levels of government, promoted "scientific philanthropy." Rather than individual almsgiving that fostered dependence and short-term solutions, practitioners advocated a new approach that encouraged independence and long-term results. Flexibility, research, and expertise were their benchmarks. By revising old patterns and refashioning familiar institutions, civic stewards and progressives alike believed that the general condition of humanity would improve. One innovation, the general-purpose foundation, overhauled long-standing traditions of private charity. Instead of "retail giving" to needy individuals, "wholesale philanthropy" advocated a more organized and rational distribution of private wealth, thereby achieving lasting public good.

In Texas after 1920, several factors converged to produce a climate conducive to the creation of philanthropic foundations. Most significantly, Spindletop, an event that dramatically altered the state's development, started an economic boom that became the linchpin of Texas prosperity. From oil profits flowed enormous revenue, lining the pockets of enterprising businessmen, as well as promoting related industries throughout the region. In the absence of state or federal regulation, hundreds of independent operators made quick fortunes in the petroleum business. As a result, by the mid-1920s Texans embarked on one of their more affluent periods, thereby securing the necessary seed money for charitably inclined men and women to sponsor philanthropic endeavors.

The preexistence of institutional antecedents, such as those created by Carnegie and Rockefeller, also promoted foundation philanthropy in Texas. With the rise of a nouveau riche class, a few civic-minded citizens sought socially acceptable and financially prudent means to dispose of their surplus income. In similar fashion to their more recognizable national peers, wealthy Texans, aware of the freestanding trust, created philanthropic organizations for scientific, religious, educational, and cultural purposes. Beginning with a scant handful of foundations during the 1920s, by mid-century donors throughout the state established approximately 180 such grant-making organizations.

The advent of urban Texas encouraged the growth of foundations as well. As a higher percentage of people moved to metropolitan areas, as economic opportunities and demands for cheap labor attracted more workers, and as political and military events such as the Mexican Revolution (1910), World War I (1917), and World War II (1941) embroiled the state in world affairs, and therefore drew more outsiders, Texas' population multiplied. Most newcomers concentrated in the major cities. With a less rural, more diverse society, Texans suffered from many of the same social afflictions of its northeastern counterparts—namely, persistent poverty, inadequate schools, and poor health care. Pernicious segregation and flagrant discrimination further compounded these problems. As a consequence, in the face of government budgetary constraints and prevailing social restrictions, as well as business and tax considerations, a substantial number of private foundations arose to address some of the unmet needs of a changing society.

Although Texas produced a few large foundations between 1920 and 1950 (see Table 7), including the Houston Endowment and the M. D. Anderson Foundation, the vast majority were modest creations, spending the bulk of their funds within the state. They were not "large bod[ies] of money completely surrounded by people who want some," as Ford Foundation scholar Dwight MacDonald famously stated. Rather, most originated as small "family affairs," with initial assets of less than $50,000. For example, The Dallas Foundation (1929) started with a meager $10,000 bequest, and the H. E. Butt Foundation (1933) originally began from the profits of a tiny Kerrville grocery store. Furthermore, they usually had limited budgets, little or no staff, and only a post office box address. First- or second-generation family members and valued business associates, many times unpaid, commonly served as trustees. Texas foundations typically contributed to local causes in or near their hometowns.

Every Texas foundation bore the mark of its creator, whether in name or design. Three early founders, Brackenridge, Hogg, and Carter (or their trustees), utilized the family moniker either to memorialize a parent, publicize a reputation, or secure permanent remembrance. Dealey and Jones, however, named their foundations to reflect their affection for a particular community, namely Dallas and Houston. Yet all supported familiar causes that they believed would benefit the people of Texas. For example, Amon Carter launched a Museum of Western Art, a reflection of his life-long interest in that region and its heritage, while Ima Hogg promoted research and education into the prevention of mental illness, a cause she had long deemed worthwhile.

Although their backgrounds and stories varied as much as the state itself, Texas donors shared certain characteristics. In general, their collective profile revealed that the majority was white, Anglo-Saxon, Protestant, and male. Few females were primary founders, while minority "donors of color" were conspicuously absent. Most were entrepreneurs, motivated not only to do good, but also to apply their business, tax, and financial acumen to their charitable endeavors. With varying degrees of wealth, all were elites, holding memberships in a small class of prominent Texas families. Many, with the exception of Ima Hogg, were first-generation nouveau riche, who were born into modest circumstances and earned their income through hard work and talent. While a few built personal monuments, many displayed a Victorian reticence about private matters; they generally preferred anonymity, agreeing to publicize their gifts only to inspire others or promote a cause. Not surprising, most of the founders were Democrats who occasionally voted Republican, and apart from school board positions did not hold elected public office. Rather, they preferred to direct events from behind the scenes or, in the case of Jesse Jones, from an appointive national post.

In addition to their homogenous makeup, the founders usually developed a unique philanthropic consciousness at an early age. Brackenridge, who had an agile mind and read broadly, approached the accumulation and distribution of his private wealth from a philosophical standpoint, supporting the doctrines of civic stewardship and Social Darwinism espoused by Carnegie and Spencer. The Progressive agenda, with its emphasis on efficiency and reform, helped shape Dealey's charitable impulse and community activities. By contrast, Jones, Hogg, and Carter, nurtured by family cultures that reinforced compassionate values, inherited their strong sense of regard for those less fortunate from their parents. For example, Ima Hogg modeled the public-spiritedness and noblesse oblige of her father, while Jesse Jones built on a long-standing tradition of generosity and service that he absorbed as a youth. All, however, approached philanthropy as a public trust attendant upon the wealthy. All articulated a social vision that stirred them deeply. All sought to return a portion of their good fortune to the communities that had enriched them. And all derived great satisfaction from their philanthropic endeavors, which gave meaning to their lives and surpassed even their great business achievements.

These wealthy citizens separated themselves from the vast majority of rich Texans by establishing a permanent vehicle for their philanthropy. By creating a grant-making foundation to distribute efficiently their surplus income "during their lifetime," as Carnegie advised, they avoided some of the public acrimony of others who died rich and, hence, "disgraced." Furthermore, they institutionalized their giving after middle age, thereby applying their substantial life experiences and accumulated disposable wealth to well-defined, long-term goals. Although several funds were not immediately activated or fully endowed, once established, most donors assumed an active philanthropic role for themselves, serving either as strategic advisors or board members. They also were more likely to be lifelong contributors, providing annual gifts or final bequests to their funds. In short, all viewed the private foundation as a superior and tangible framework to channel their private wealth both for business purposes and for the public good.

Despite the many similarities, Texas foundation philanthropists also differed in important ways. For example, only Ima Hogg and Amon Carter were native-born Texans; all others were out-of-state transplants who profited from the seemingly boundless opportunities within the state, and then returned a portion of their wealth to their adopted communities. Ambitious, self-reliant, and adventurous, they built diverse empires from cotton, oil, lumber, construction, banking, publishing, and real estate. Their educational backgrounds varied as well, from elementary and secondary schools to business colleges and universities. What some lacked in formal training, they made up for in ability, perseverance, and vision. While three of the five founders examined in this volume married, only Dealey and Carter left children to inherit a portion of their estates, thereby providing a generational link to their original philanthropic intent. Without direct descendants, Brackenridge, Jones, and Hogg—much like Carnegie, who was childless—relied instead on trusted associates to disburse much of their wealth for its intended purposes.

Texas women, constrained by law and custom, played a less prominent role as philanthropic donors. Even Andrew Carnegie dismissed women as potential benefactors when he referred to the "man of means." Nevertheless, they were active participants, albeit in reduced numbers. Although exact figures are unavailable, of the 214 institutions listed in the 1960 *Foundation Directory*, fifty-four women jointly established foundations with their spouses; only nine acted independently. Their male counterparts may have earned fortunes through entrepreneurship, but, typically, female activists such as Ima Hogg inherited their wealth or, in the case of Nenetta Carter, were conscripted into service by their husbands. Nevertheless, most had already been involved in charitable and volunteer activities in their communities. They therefore understood firsthand the need for long-term solutions, rather than purely ameliorative Band-Aids, as well as the tax advantages afforded to organized giving. These women, once engaged in philanthropy, usually were active donors, bringing an enlarged social consciousness and a unique set of values to their commitments, such as mental health, childcare, and female education. Moreover, because few females had the financial resources to fund a foundation, many found meaningful work within the sector, outside the traditional roles of teacher or nurse. For example, Maud Keeling assumed the post of CSF executive director, while Katrine Deakins and Ruth Carter Stevenson acquired board positions with the Carter Foundation. Organized philanthropy, therefore, provided an avenue for socially conscious Texas women to assume leadership roles and to exercise public influence through private wealth.

By their very nature, early Texas foundations were elitist institutions. Their philanthropic goals and grant-making decisions were determined by those with the greatest resources, namely wealthy Texans. Consequently, they became de facto policy makers, shaping vital decisions concerning the sick, the underprivileged, and the needy. Nevertheless, the causes to which individuals have left their money often provide a window to the needs, values, and priorities of a society. An analysis of the fields of interest of early Texas foundations confirmed this premise. From 1920 to 1950 wealthy Texans devoted approximately 50 percent of all foundation dollars to predetermined purposes such as educational, religious, and community endeavors. (See Table 6.) These benefactions represented an important cultural index, reflecting many of the issues and concerns of early-twentieth-century Texans.

The area of education, in particular college and university training, provided the greatest opportunity for service. Neglected by the federal government and only marginally supported by the state, it received the highest share of foundation attention, or approximately 19.1 percent. Many donors, unable to complete their own schooling, especially valued learning as an avenue for personal advancement. Furthermore, they accepted as axiomatic that mass education, as Thomas Jefferson advised, produced a more responsible citizenry, thereby providing "ladders for the aspiring to rise." Accordingly, when they decided to institutionalize their philanthropy, wealthy Texans funded "Brackenridge scholars," established Jesse and Mary Jones free libraries, and provided Amon Carter Jr. college scholarships to worthy students.

Religious support and community welfare were also popular fields of interest for early Texas foundations. As the only recipient entirely dependent on voluntary giving, religion—especially Protestant and Jewish faiths—received 15.6 percent of foundation dollars. Why? First of all, while Catholics remained the single largest denomination in the state, Protestants and Jews comprised the majority of Texas congregations. Their religious leaders traditionally emphasized the importance of stewardship, which resulted in members of these faiths creating most of the early foundations. Second, church attendance increased statewide, especially after the depression years, thereby focusing more attention on moral responsibilities and charitable duties. Finally, the accelerated changes brought on by modernization and urbanization led to a resurgence in religious fundamentalism during the 1920s. One avenue for affluent Baptists and evangelical Methodists in the South to preserve rural values, disseminate the gospel, and finance missionary undertakings was to channel their private wealth through philanthropic foundations committed to those ends.

At the same time, social and community programs garnered a significant portion of assistance with 14.3 percent. Not surprising, Texas foundations, with broad, open-ended charitable missions, responded to many of the economic and social exigencies created by the Great Depression, the rise of urban Texas, and the outbreak of two world wars. Due to rising poverty, crowded cities, reduced educational opportunities, few cultural or recreational facilities, and inadequate health care, they increasingly assumed greater responsibilities to augment government efforts. Furthermore, many founders were grateful citizens who had risen to the top financially and desired to make recompense to benefit their hometowns. They therefore approved grants to improve local neighborhoods, expand human services, and provide social welfare programs "for the people of Texas."

While the sizes of their philanthropic gifts varied, most resulted, either directly or indirectly, from oil revenues. For example, Ima Hogg and Amon Carter funded their foundations by using money gained from the petroleum industry. Jesse Jones and George Dealey benefited financially from the businesses spurred by Spindletop—construction, finance, and publishing. Even George Brackenridge, who died in 1920 before the oil boom peaked, received some residual benefits through his banking and real estate holdings. Moreover, in 1923, when oil was discovered on University of Texas lands—property that he had managed as regent—he not only posthumously helped secure the future of the Austin campus but also assured his own educational legacy.

Yet the early record of organized philanthropy in Texas did not address the immediate social and racial problems facing the state. Wealthy donors typically channeled their funds into long-term solutions, such as education and research, or into community enhancement like museums and parks, rather than direct relief that mitigated symptoms but afforded little permanent change. Most also did not use their wealth or position to challenge the status quo, which in Jim Crow Texas meant segregation, discrimination, even lynching. Rather, foundation philanthropists used their resources to assist minorities within the prevailing class system of "separate but equal" facilities. For instance, Brackenridge aided historically black colleges; Jones assisted black churches and schools; and Carter financed improvements at segregated parks.

During the cold war years (1945–70) Texas foundations, like their national counterparts, did not escape public scrutiny or congressional inquiry. The vast accumulation of private wealth in the coffers of a few autonomous grant-making institutions aroused the ire both of Populist critics and financial watchdogs. With their tax-exempt status and self-perpetuating boards of directors, private foundations functioned as exclusive clubs with unusual social and cultural hegemony. Furthermore, they operated behind a shroud of secrecy and without governmental constraints. As a consequence, beginning in the 1950s, the U.S. Congress undertook several investigations into their unparalleled power and political influence. During the 1960s, when public confidence in American institutions declined, the Patman committee held hearings concerning their questionable grant making and financial operations. His congressional probe targeted both the Houston and Carter foundations, as well as several other large Texas funds. This sustained attack culminated in the passage of the Tax Reform Act of 1969, which had a chilling effect on Texas foundations, placing them under strict federal oversight and curbing many of their previously unregulated practices.

By 1970, foundation philanthropy in Texas had reached a turning point. No longer would donors and their motives remain sacrosanct and unchallenged. No longer would tax-exempt funds, designated for philanthropic purposes, be jeopardized by improper financial practices. No longer would foundations control ownership in family or corporate businesses. Changing attitudes had transformed government policy, and a new era of public accountability and wider accessibility had commenced, thereby redefining the world of organized philanthropy.

Despite their shortcomings, private foundations and their donors have played significant roles in the economic, social, and cultural development of Texas. By funding medical research, establishing educational scholarships, building public libraries, financing art museums, and supporting community projects, they have helped bridge the gap between the "haves" and the "have nots." Recognition of these modern pioneers, like their nineteenth-century ancestors, will help broaden the stereotypical image of individualistic, combative Texans, thus providing additional insight into the Texas character. Their legacy to the people of Texas has been the voluntary, purposeful use of private wealth for the public good.

EPILOGUE
Looking Backward

AT THE END OF THE TWENTIETH CENTURY, Julian West, the fictitious young time traveler in Edward Bellamy's *Looking Backward, 2000–1887* (published in 1888), grimly contrasted the bleak conditions of the late nineteenth century with the utopian social order of the new millennium. In this new "Golden Age," the author postulated, the state owned the means of production, and all citizens shared equally in the accumulation and distribution of wealth. Although the "perfect society" that Bellamy described one year prior to the publication of Carnegie's "Wealth" failed to materialize, attempts to "improve the condition of mankind," whether through individual effort, government programs, or organized philanthropy, have persisted to the present day.

Borrowing a page from this imaginative, yet provocative novel—but with the advantage of historical hindsight—what does a look backward from the present to 1970 reveal? Specifically, how have Texas foundations fared during the regulatory era? What changes have ushered in the modern era of private philanthropy?

In this most recent, fifth stage of development, yet another new period in organized giving emerged. Initially, start-up foundations declined in the wake of the Tax Reform Act of 1969. Weakened tax incentives and negative asset growth from the new legislation, as well as shrinking resources from the financial market collapse of 1973–74, resulted in a decrease in new philanthropic organizations. With the surge in oil prices in the mid-1970s, however, petroleum revenues once again encouraged institutional philanthropy. According to the 1982 *Directory of Texas Foundations,* Texas donors founded 950 more foundations. After 1983, when oil rates dropped precipitously and the Texas economy stagnated, contributions to grant-making institutions fell. Not until a decade later, with the added stimulation of electronics and "high-tech" computer plants, did the recession ebb, thereby creating a younger, more socially diverse class of wealthy Texans. This new generation of civic-minded nouveau riche applied the same kind of entrepreneurial drive and public-spiritedness to their "getting" and "giving" as did the early pioneers. Yet they created their foundations at a much earlier age and, more importantly, while they were still building their financial empires. As a consequence, between 1982 and 2000 the latest directory listed an additional 1,718 private foundations, an increase of over 100 percent.

Despite the corrective provisions of the Tax Reform Act of 1969, Texas foundations over the last thirty years have not always conducted their affairs as if they were public trusts. Many still do not issue annual reports or provide detailed grant-making criteria. Some continue to guard closely their privacy and are reluctant to open their files and records. And others, while meeting the letter of the law, remain divided on the wisdom of the Tax Reform Act, conceding its necessary reforms, while decrying its deleterious effects on financial contributions and foundation births.

Nevertheless, after 1970 a basic philosophical shift occurred in the Texas foundation community. Many organizations became less secretive, even self-promotional, seeking to educate the public about their good work. Increasingly, they issued program guidelines, published newsletters, and established web pages. Foundation directories, annual reports, and community meetings aided their increased visibility as well. Foundations also became more responsible to their constituents, forming partnerships and establishing relationships with their grantees. Rather than a "top-down" management style, foundations began to emphasize a more "bottom-up," less elitist approach, thereby hoping to forestall future congressional inquiries and foster goodwill.

Professionalization in the foundation world continued apace. In the new era of accountability, trustees required a paid, trained staff to administer expenses, monitor reporting requirements, and maintain fiscal responsibility. Toward those ends, new philanthropic careers became necessary to ensure proper foundation management. Accordingly, executive directors with professional experience, program officers, staff accountants, and financial advisors filled these new openings within private philanthropy. This new cadre of grant-making professionals replaced or augmented family members at many Texas foundations, bringing more objective criteria to grant-making practices.

Beginning in the 1970s more women and minorities began to occupy the ranks of professional positions within Texas foundations as well. Many from these groups entered organized philanthropy through the nonprofit career path. Mirroring national trends of affirmative action and efforts toward more diversity, foundations employed more female and minority staff members—often in excess of national averages and other professions.

Grant-making criteria evolved as well. Responding to the changing socio-economic and demographic trends in Texas, such as an aging population, awakened minorities, and increased globalization, many trustees reduced funding for traditional brick and mortar projects in favor of more social and health services. At the same time, as government funding for the arts and cultural institutions waned, foundation support for creative activities tripled. Many grant-making organizations during the post-1969 era committed their resources to maintaining symphony orchestras, ballet troupes, theater companies, and art galleries. They also adopted a willingness to take risks with their philanthropic dollars by supporting new models of giving. For example, foundations financed experimental pilot programs and advocated innovative approaches to unsolved problems. At the same time, a new breed of goal-oriented donors promoted "social venture philanthropy"—the application of business expertise to the nonprofit sector—with expectations of tangible results from their gifts. While most continued to give to predetermined unsolicited projects, secondary and higher education, cultural endeavors, and human services received the largest share of Texas foundation dollars during this fifth stage.

Philanthropic institutions, similar to many family businesses, also have, in some cases, undergone predictable life cycles: success during the reign of the founder, stagnation under second-generation leadership, and then termination when grandchildren exhibit little interest in perpetuating the legacy. Yet all of the organizations included in this book have successfully maintained and enlarged upon their charitable missions. Decades after the donors' deaths, their original intent "to benefit the people of Texas" endures. The Houston Endowment continues to rank as the largest in the state (and twenty-ninth nationwide) with assets of $1.3 billion and provides grants of over $53 million to benefit Texas citizens. The Amon Carter Foundation, eleventh in size with $270 million in assets, appropriates approximately 45 percent of its grants to support the cultural and performing arts in Fort Worth. With $103 million, the Hogg Foundation for Mental Health, the thirty-fourth largest in the state, remains faithful to its donor's wishes and is one of the outstanding philanthropic leaders in the Southwest. Representing community foundations, the fastest-growing sector of private philanthropy, is The Dallas Foundation, ranked forty-second overall with over $85 million. The Brackenridge Foundation, now more than eighty years old, holds assets of approximately $29 million and is the ninety-eighth largest in the state. And the Conference of Southwest Foundations, which recently celebrated its half century mark, continues to hold annual meetings, which currently accommodate approximately 230 active members, some of whom represent minority foundations.

So as Texas enters the new millennium, as more citizens accumulate wealth from emerging information and computer technology, and as aging baby boomers prepare for the largest generational transfer of wealth, estimated between $41 and $136 trillion nationwide, Texans are uniquely positioned to create unprecedented philanthropic capital. Whether and how they leverage their private wealth for the public good is the major question for the twenty-first century.

APPENDIX

TABLE 1
Early Texas Foundations, 1920–50

FOUNDATION	CITY	DATE
George W. Brackenridge	San Antonio	1920
Pauline Sterne Wolff	Houston	1922
Sealy and Smith	Galveston	1922
William Buchanan	Texarkana	1923
Luling	Luling	1927
Sunnyside	Dallas	1928
Graham Benevolent	Graham	1928
Adolph Schwartz	El Paso	1928
Dallas Community Trust	Dallas	1929
Baptist	Dallas	1930
Rockwell Fund	Houston	1931
Overbid Property Trust	Aransas Pass	1931
Howard E. Butt	Corpus Christi	1933
Clayton	Houston	1933
Bessie I. Hoffstetter	Corsicana	1934
Less Privileged H F Account	Wichita Falls	1934
Ruth Cohen Frisch	Galveston	1934*
Hardin	Wichita Falls	1934
Daniel and Edith Ripley	Houston	1935*
LeTourneau	Longview	1935*
Fleming	Fort Worth	1936*
R. W. Fair	Tyler	1936
Longview	Longview	1936
Kimball	Fort Worth	1936
Newby Memorial	Fort Worth	1936
M. D. Anderson	Houston	1936
Mary L. Peyton	El Paso	1937
Houston Endowment, Inc.	Houston	1937*
Fohs	Houston	1937
Gonzales Warm Springs	Gonzales	1937
West	Houston	1938
Navarro Community	Corsicana	1938
Westervelt Trust	Corpus Christi	1938
B. A. and Elinor Steinhagen	Beaumont	1939
Mutual Benefit	Houston	1939
Dreyfuss	Dallas	1939*
Southwest Medical	Dallas	1939*
Storey	Dallas	1939

TABLE 1 (CONTINUED)
Early Texas Foundations, 1920–50

FOUNDATION	CITY	DATE
Hogg	Austin	1940
S. F. Cowles	Wichita Falls	1940*
Hall-Voyer	Honey Grove	1940
David Graham Hall	Dallas	1940*
Dougherty	Beeville	1940
Joe and Lois Perkins	Wichita Falls	1941*
Harriet Mosher Memorial Fund	Dallas	1941
Southwest Research	San Antonio	1941
Texas Natural Resources	San Antonio	1941
D. K. Caldwell	Tyler	1941
Hoblitzelle	Dallas	1942
Moody	Galveston	1942
Rupe	Dallas	1942
Fain	Wichita Falls	1942*
Bible Tract and Missionary Society	Sugar Land	1942
Brown and Lupton	Fort Worth	1942*
Wolens	Corsicana	1942*
W. B. Munson	Denison	1943
Forrest	Lubbock	1943
Weingarten Welfare	Houston	1943
Pryor Charitable	San Antonio	1943
Cooper	Waco	1943
Children's Memorial Fund	San Antonio	1943*
Blakley-Braniff	Dallas	1943
Hal and Charlie Peterson	Kerrville	1944
Flora B. Cameron	Waco	1944
Adams Best	Austin	1944
Battelstein Charities	Houston	1944
J. W. and Cornelia R. Scarbrough	Austin	1944*
Lemuel Scarbrough	Austin	1944*
Lichtenstein	Corpus Christi	1944
Oxsheer Smith	Cameron	1944*
William and Catherine Bryce	Fort Worth	1944
Fenton J. Baker	Dallas	1944
Lack	Houston	1944
Bass	Fort Worth	1945
Amon G. Carter	Fort Worth	1945
Montgomery	Hidalgo County	1945
William Bryce	Fort Worth	1945
O. P. Hairgrove	Houston	1945
Max Krost	Houston	1945
Amon Carter S-T Employees	Fort Worth	1945

TABLE 1 (CONTINUED)
Early Texas Foundations, 1920–50

FOUNDATION	CITY	DATE
Chilton	Dallas	1945
Mossler Corporation	Houston	1945*
J. R. P.	Dallas	1945
Neiman-Marcus Company	Dallas	1945
Driscoll	Corpus Christi	1945
Fair	Fort Worth	1945
George	Richmond	1945
Hobby	Houston	1945*
Plitt Southern Theaters Employees	Dallas	1945
Mary Mosher Belden	Dallas	1945
Texarkana Youth	Texarkana	1945*
Rooke	Woodsboro	1945*
Leo Potishman	Fort Worth	1945*
Kuykendall	Lubbock	1946
J. Newton Rayzor	Houston	1946
Berlowitz	Houston	1946
Steves	San Antonio	1946
Charles H. Harris	Fort Worth	1946
Ora C. Forrest	Slaton	1946
Harris and Eliza Kempner Fund	Galveston	1946
Runnells	Bay City	1946
Alice G. K. Kleberg	Kingsville	1946
King Ranch Family	Kingsville	1946
Earl C. Sams	Corpus Christi	1946
Feldman	Dallas	1946
Rudman	Tyler	1946
Perry	Robstown	1946
Texas Research	Renner	1946
Curtis	Longview	1946*
Cullen	Houston	1947
Foley Brothers	Houston	1947
S. Brachmans Fund	Fort Worth	1947*
Mary and John O'Brian Shary	Mission	1947*
Vaughn	San Antonio	1947*
Gray	Houston	1947*
Sid Richardson	Fort Worth	1947*
Finger	Houston	1947*
Harding	Raymondville	1947*
W. P. & Bulah Luse	Dallas	1947
Lulu Bryan Rambaud	Houston	1947
Runnells Fund	Wharton	1947
Frank Wood	Wichita Falls	1947*

TABLE 1 (CONTINUED)
Early Texas Foundations, 1920–50

FOUNDATION	CITY	DATE
S. Brachmans Fund	Fort Worth	1947*
Scanlan	Houston	1947*
John W. and Nellie Akin	Longview	1948
Morris and Birdie Rauch	Houston	1948
Jack and Katherine Pearce	Galveston	1948
Ed Cox	Dallas	1948
Carl J. Aldenhoven	Fort Worth	1948*
Fondren	Houston	1948
Senior Citizens	Dallas	1948
E. D. Farmer	Dallas	1948
McGaha	Wichita Falls	1948
B. W. Trull	Palacios	1948
Susan V. Clayton Slum Clearance	Houston	1948
M. N. Davidson	Houston	1948*
Meadows	Dallas	1948*
Dora Roberts	Fort Worth	1948
B. M. Woltman	Houston	1948
Louise Lindsley Merrick	Bandera	1948
Egmont S. Smith	Temple	1948*
Edna Gladney	Houston	1948*
Oldham Little Church	Houston	1949
Mary Moore Mcmillan	Overton	1949
Rockwell Fund	Houston	1949*
E. B. Mohr	Dallas	1949*
Constantin	Dallas	1949
Russell	Houston	1949
Mary E. Bivins	Amarillo	1949*
Texas Educational Association	Fort Worth	1949*
J. S. Bridwell	Wichita Falls	1949*
Bertner	Houston	1949
McManis Mission	Houston	1949
Goldston	Houston	1949
Earl Hayes	Dallas	1949*
George	Richmond	1949
Scott, Sherwood & Brindley	Temple	1949
Diamond M	Snyder	1949
Hatton	Dallas	1949
Robert J. and Helen C. Kleberg	San Antonio	1950*
Minnie Stevens Piper	San Antonio	1950*
Mullen	Alice	1950
Herman P. Taubman	Dallas	1950
Germany	Dallas	1950

TABLE 1 (CONTINUED)
Early Texas Foundations, 1920–50

FOUNDATION	CITY	DATE
Tellepsen	Houston	1950
Arthur C. Hughes	Dallas	1950
Alvin M. and Lucy B. Owsley	Dallas	1950
Winship	Clarkwood	1950
Wald-Hirsch	Houston	1950
James R. Dougherty Jr.	Beeville	1950
Biological Humanics	Dallas	1950
William Clay Jr.	Fort Worth	1950*
Eldon Durrett Memorial	Amarillo	1950
Earl Hayes	Dallas	1950
Lackey Memorial	Fort Worth	1950
Meyer and Ida Gordon	Houston	1950*
Haggar	Dallas	1950
Laurent	Houston	1950
	Total:	178

*Date of incorporation

Due to fragmentary records, no complete listing of early Texas foundations exists. Table 1 is a compilation from several sources: Conference of Southwest Foundations, *Preliminary Directory*, Box 2.325/V116a, File Preliminary Directory of Texas Foundations and Trust Funds, CSFP; Wilmer Shields Rich, ed., *American Foundations and Their Fields* (7th ed.; New York: Raymond Rich Associates and Marts and Lundy, Inc., 1955); Walton and Andrews, eds., *The Foundation Directory;* Ann D. Walton and Marianna O. Lewis, eds. *The Foundation Directory* (2d ed.; New York: Russell Sage Foundation, 1964); Marianna O. Lewis, ed., *The Foundation Directory* (3d ed.; New York: Russell Sage Foundation, 1967); Lewis and Bowers, eds., *The Foundation Directory;* William T. Hooper Jr., ed., *Directory of Texas Foundations* (Austin: n.p., 1975); *Conference of Southwest Foundations, 1949–1998: Fiftieth Anniversary* (Austin: n.p., 1998).

TABLE 2
Periods of Origin of Early Texas Foundations, 1920–50

PERIOD	NUMBER	PERCENT
1920–24	4	2.23
1925–29	5	2.8
1930–34	9	5.03
1935–39	20	11.17
1940–44	35	19.55
1945–50	105	59.22
Total:	178	100

Statistics based on Table 1, which includes all known foundations from 1920 to 1950. The period 1945–50 included six years, while all others have five. Note that Table 3 covers a larger date range, but includes only those foundations with a minimum level of assets.

TABLE 3

Periods of Origin of Early Texas Foundations by Decades, 1920–69

PERIOD	NUMBER	PERCENT
1920–29	4	2
1930–39	14	6
1940–49	50	20
1950–59	114	46
1960–69	65	26
Total:	247	100

The first edition of *The Foundation Directory* (1960) included only those Texas foundations with assets of $50,000 or more and with grants of at least $10,000 in the latest year of record. The fourth edition (1971) of the directory listed Texas foundations with assets of $500,000 or more and grants totaling at least $25,000 a year. Lewis and Bowers, eds., *The Foundation Directory*, pp. xii–xiii.

TABLE 4

Geographical Distribution of Early Texas Foundations by Regions, 1920–50

REGION	NUMBER	PERCENT
Central Texas	14	7.8
Northeast Texas	80	44.7
Southeast Texas	51	29
West Texas	2	1.1
Coastal Bend	11	6.1
Panhandle	6	3.4
South Texas	14	7.8
Total:	178	100

Statistics based on Table 1. Due to rounding, figures approximate 100 percent.

TABLE 5

Geographical Distribution of Early Texas Foundations by Cities, 1920–50

CITY	NUMBER	PERCENT
Houston	39	22.3
Dallas	35	19.6
Fort Worth	21	11.7
San Antonio	8	4.5
Wichita Falls	7	3.9
Corpus Christi	5	2.9
Austin	5	2.8
Galveston	5	2.8

TABLE 5 (CONTINUED)
Geographical Distribution of Early Texas Foundations by Cities, 1920–50

CITY	NUMBER	PERCENT
Longview	4	2.2
Corsicana	3	1.7
Tyler	3	1.7
Texarkana	2	1.1
Lubbock	2	1.1
Richmond	2	1.1
Amarillo	2	1.1
Kingsville	2	1.1
Beeville	2	1.1
Waco	2	1.1
El Paso	2	1.1
Temple	2	1.1
Luling	1	.5
Graham	1	.5
Aransas Pass	1	.5
Denison	1	.5
Bay City	1	.5
Raymondville	1	.5
Palacios	1	.5
Clarkwood	1	.5
Kerrville	1	.5
Honey Grove	1	.5
Gonzales	1	.5
Beaumont	1	.5
Sugar Land	1	.5
Woodsboro	1	.5
Robstown	1	.5
Renner	1	.5
Wharton	1	.5
Mission	1	.5
Bandera	1	.5
Overton	1	.5
Hidalgo County	1	.5
Cameron	1	.5
Slaton	1	.5
Snyder	1	.5
Alice	1	.5
Total:	178	100

Statistics based on Table 1. Due to rounding, figures approximate 100 percent.

TABLE 6

Distribution of Early Texas Foundations by Fields, 1920–50

FIELDS	PERCENT
Aged	2.5
Animal Related	.3
Arts/Cultural	4.7
Child Welfare/Youth	11.8
Civic Activities	1.5
Community Improvement/Social Welfare	14.3
Education	19.1
Employees	.9
Environment	.9
Food/Nutrition/Agriculture	1.5
Health/Hospitals	13.0
Housing/Shelter	1.2
Individual Relief	5.1
Legal Aid	.6
Mental Health	1.5
Science/Medicine/Research	5.7
Recreation	.6
Religion	15.6
Total:	100

Percentages based on averages of reported foundation purposes and activities. Due to rounding, figures approximate 100 percent. Walton and Andrews, eds., *The Foundation Directory*, pp. 613–37.

TABLE 7

Top Ten Early Texas Foundations by Assets, 1958

FOUNDATION	CITY	ASSETS*
1. Robert A. Welch	Houston	$50
2. M. D. Anderson	Houston	$37
3. Houston Endowment	Houston	$35
4. Amon Carter	Fort Worth	$16
5. Clayton Foundation for Research	Houston	$9
6. Hoblitzelle	Dallas	$8
7. Hogg	Austin	$6.5
8. Minnie Stevens Piper	San Antonio	$4.5
9. LeTourneau	Longview	$3.95
10. Schlumberger	Houston	$3.92

*in millions

The Welch Foundation was established in 1954 and M. D. Anderson was founded in 1936. After 1962 the Houston Endowment became the largest foundation in the state. Walton and Andrews, eds., *The Foundation Directory*, pp. 613–37.

NOTES

Introduction

1. F. Emerson Andrews, an early authority on organized philanthropy, defined a foundation as "a nongovernmental, nonprofit organization having a principal fund of its own, managed by its own trustees or directors, and established to maintain or aid social, educational, charitable, religious, or other activities serving the common welfare." Several early philanthropic institutions existed prior to the twentieth century that possessed some of the characteristics of a modern foundation; however, donors used various names for their endeavors, such as the Benjamin Franklin Fund (1789), the Magdalen Society (1800), the Smithsonian Institution (1846) and the Peabody Education Fund (1867). Carnegie established a few early specific gifts including the Carnegie Foundation for Advancement of Teaching (1905) and the Carnegie Endowment for International Peace (1910). He also founded the Carnegie Corporation of New York in 1911—his first general-purpose foundation. Rockefeller created the Rockefeller Foundation in 1913. See Robert H. Wiebe, *The Search for Order, 1877–1920*. See also F. Emerson Andrews, *Philanthropic Foundations,* p. 11.
2. John D. Rockefeller, *Random Reminiscences of Men and Events,* p. 156; and Frederick T. Gates, *Chapters in My Life,* p. 277.
3. Exact figures for the number of foundations nationwide are incomplete. Statistics refer to mid-size and large foundations. See Ann D. Walton and F. Emerson Andrews, eds., *The Foundation Directory;* Andrews, *Philanthropic Foundations,* pp. 11–13; and Lester M. Salamon, *America's Nonprofit Sector: A Primer,* pp. 10–11.
4. John Winthrop, "A Modell of Christian Charity," *Settlements to Society, 1584–1763,* ed. by Jack P. Greene, pp. 66–69; and Robert H. Bremner, *American Philanthropy,* pp. 5–18.
5. Warren Weaver, *U.S. Philanthropic Foundations: Their History, Structure, Management, and Record,* pp. 19–26; and Kathleen D. McCarthy, *Noblesse Oblige: Charity & Cultural Philanthropy in Chicago, 1849–1929,* p. ix.
6. Constitution, amend. 10; and Alexis de Tocqueville, *Democracy in America,* vol. 2, ed. by J. P. Mayer and Max Lerner, p. 485.
7. Tocqueville, *Democracy in America,* vol. 2, p. 546; and James Bryce, *The American Commonwealth,* vol. 2, pp. 875–77.
8. Arthur M. Schlesinger Sr., "The True American Way of Life," *St. Louis Post-Dispatch,* Dec. 13, 1953, sec. 2, p. 3; Merle Curti, "American Philanthropy and the National Character," *American Quarterly* 10 (fall, 1958): 420–24; and Merle Curti, "The History of American Philanthropy as a Field of Research," *American Historical Association* 62 (Jan., 1957): 352.
9. 1 Cor. 13:13 KJV; and Weaver, *U.S. Philanthropic Foundations,* p. 5.
10. An English critic named the article the "Gospel of Wealth" to distinguish it from the "Gospel of Christianity." Andrew Carnegie, "Wealth," *North American Review* 148 (June, 1889): 660–63; Rockefeller, *Random Reminiscences,* pp. 141–42; Bremner, *American Philanthropy,* p. 3; and Jan Van Til, et al., *Critical Issues in American Philanthropy,* pp. 19–34.
11. Walton and Andrews, eds., *The Foundation Directory,* pp. xix–xx; and James Allen Smith, "The Evolving American Foundation," *Philanthropy and the Nonprofit Sector in a Changing America,* ed. by Charles T. Clotfelter and Thomas Ehrlich, pp. 36–37.
12. See M. M. Chambers, *Charters of Philanthropies: A Study of Selected Trust Instruments, Charters, By-Laws, and Court Decisions.*
13. *The Foundation Directory* (1960) utilized the definition by F. Emerson Andrews to compile

its information. Furthermore, using 1958 data, the directory included only those funds with assets of $50,000 or more and with grants totaling at least $10,000 a year. Despite these early efforts, accurate and complete data on early foundations were fragmentary. The general research foundations (178) and independent foundations (3,006) were combined to total 3,184. Special purpose foundations comprised the category "operating foundations." Walton and Andrews, eds., *The Foundation Directory*, pp. ix–xxv; Andrews, *Philanthropic Foundations*, p. 11; and Salamon, *America's Nonprofit Sector*, pp. 26–28.

14. Benjamin Disraeli, *Vivian Grey*, vol. 1, p. ix; Simon Kuznets, "Long Term Changes in the National Income of the United States Since 1870," *Income and Wealth of the United States, Trends and Structures*, vol. 2, pp. 50–55; Gates, *Chapters in My Life*, pp. 205–15; and Ben Whitaker, *The Philanthropoids: Foundations and Society*, p. 65.

15. Carnegie, "Wealth," pp. 653–64; Gates, *Chapters in My Life*, p. 206; Margaret Olivia Sage, "Opportunities and Responsibilities of Leisured Women," *North American Review* 181 (Nov., 1905): 712–21; Merle Curti, Judith Green, and Roderick Nash, "Anatomy of Giving: Millionaires in the Late 19th Century," *American Quarterly* 15 (1963): 416–35; Richard L. Heilbroner, *The Making of Economic Society*, pp. 104–105; and Smith, "The Evolving American Foundation," p. 40.

16. Walton and Andrews, eds., *The Foundation Directory*, pp. x–xiii; and Smith, "The Evolving American Foundation," p. 40.

17. Peter Dobkin Hall, "A Historical Overview of the Private Nonprofit Sector," *The Nonprofit Sector: A Research Handbook*, ed. by Walter W. Powell, pp. 17–18; and Smith, "The Evolving American Foundation," p. 40.

18. Because the two directories used different criteria, exact numerical comparisons are not valid. Nevertheless, an explosive growth in foundations occurred, especially from 1945 to 1960. See Wilmer Shields Rich and Neva R. Deardorff, eds., *American Foundations and Their Fields*; Walton and Andrews, eds., *The Foundation Directory*, p. x; Marianna O. Lewis and Patricia Bowers, eds., *The Foundation Directory*, p. vii; and Tax Reform Act of 1969, *Statutes at Large* 83 (1970): 487.

19. Alwyn Barr, "The Other Texas: Charities and Community in the Lone Star State," *Southwestern Historical Quarterly* 97 (July, 1993): 1; and Peggy Hildreth, "Howard Associations," *The New Handbook of Texas*, ed. by Ron Tyler, et al., vol. 3, pp. 747–48.

20. Robert Sutherland, interview by Graham Blackstock, Oct. 30, 1971, Box 3M361, File: Talk Notes: Austin, Texas, Oct. 30, 1971, Taped interview, Robert Sutherland Papers, Center for American History, Austin (hereafter referred to as RSP); Barr, "The Other Texas," pp. 3, 6; and Walton and Andrews, *The Foundation Directory*, pp. 613–37.

21. See Appendix, Tables 1 and 2. Walton and Andrews, eds., *The Foundation Directory*, pp. xviii, 613–37.

22. See Appendix, Tables 1–3. Walton and Andrews, eds., *The Foundation Directory*, pp. xviii, 619.

23. See Appendix, Tables 1–3. Walton and Andrews, eds., *The Foundation Directory*, pp. xviii, 624; and Hall, "The Historical Overview of the Nonprofit Sector," pp. 15–18.

24. See Appendix, Tables 1–3. Aris A. Mallas Jr., "Recent Trends Affecting Southwest Foundations," Box 2.325/V116a, File: 1956, Eighth Annual Conference of Southwest Foundations, Corpus Christi, Tex., Apr. 12–13, 1956, Conference of Southwest Foundations Papers, Center for American History, Austin (hereafter referred to as CSFP); Walton and Andrews, eds., *The Foundation Directory*, p. 616; Lewis and Bowers, eds., *The Foundation Directory*, pp. xi–xiii; and Tax Reform Act of 1969, *Statutes at Large* 83 (1970): 487.

25. The U.S. Census reported Texas population growth as 6,414,842 in 1940, rising to 7,111,194 in 1950, and then 9,579,611 in 1960. Urban dwellers increased from 45 to 62.7

to 75 percent. See *U.S. Census Statistical Abstract of the United States: 1940, 1950, 1960.* See also Table 4 for geographical distribution of Texas foundations. Sutherland interview, RSP; Walton and Andrews, eds., *The Foundation Directory,* pp. xviii–xix; and Hall, "A Historical Overview of the Private Nonprofit Sector," p. 18.

Chapter 1

1. Brackenridge was buried in the family cemetery near Edna in Jackson County. A final inventory of the estate revealed his fortune to be less than $1.5 million. See *San Antonio Express,* Dec. 26, 1921, p. 6; "Two Interesting Wills," *The Alcalde* 10 (Nov., 1922): 1518–19; Roy Bedichek, "The Patron Saint of the University of Texas," *The Alcalde* 5 (Apr., 1917): 480–86; and Marilyn McAdams Sibley, *George W. Brackenridge: Maverick Philanthropist,* p. 245.
2. *San Antonio Express,* Dec. 26, 1921, through January 2, 1922, carried a complete transcript of the will, lawsuit, and testimony. See "In Re Estate George W. Brackenridge, Deceased," Brief for the Appellees No. 6814, Court of Civil Appeals for the Fourth Supreme Judicial District of Texas, San Antonio, 1921. Robert E. Vinson, "The University Crosses the Bar," *Southwestern Historical Quarterly* 40 (Jan., 1940): 292; and Bedichek, "The Patron Saint," pp. 480–86ff.
3. Like his second will, Brackenridge's personal papers, with the exception of a few documents, have been lost or destroyed. "Two Interesting Wills," p. 1517; and Sibley, *George W. Brackenridge,* pp. 247, 253–54.
4. *Austin American,* Jan. 5, 1921, p. 1; July 19, 1936, p. 2; "Two Interesting Wills," p. 1520; and Sibley, *George W. Brackenridge,* p. 254.
5. Only a few foundations existed in the first two decades of the twentieth century—but none in Texas. For a listing of early Texas foundations, 1920–50, see Appendix, Table 1. *San Antonio Express,* Jan. 14, 1912, p. 12A; Dec. 29, 1921, p. 6; A. W. Terrell, "Address of Judge A. W. Terrell, of Austin, Presenting the Portrait of Colonel Brackenridge," *The Alcalde* 1 (Apr., 1913): 103–106ff; "Two Interesting Wills," p. 1519; Bedichek, "The Patron Saint," pp. 481–83; Andrew Carnegie, *Autobiography of Andrew Carnegie,* pp. 255–269ff; and Sibley, *George W. Brackenridge,* pp. 15–16.
6. The Civil War divided the Brackenridge family: three brothers fought in the Confederate army while George, a Unionist, served with the U.S. Treasury Department. See Carnegie, "Wealth," p. 662; *Population of the United States in 1860; Compiled from Original Returns of the Eighth Census,* p. 487; *San Antonio Express,* Dec. 29, 1920, p. 1; *The Brackenridge Foundation: Fifty Years of Philanthropy, 1920–1970,* p. 4; Carnegie, *Autobiography,* pp. 1–18ff; and "George Washington Brackenridge," *New Handbook of Texas,* vol. 1, pp. 689–90.
7. George Brackenridge to Alexander W. Terrell, Oct. 1, 1919, Box 2H12, Alexander W. Terrell Papers, Center for American History, University of Texas, Austin (hereafter cited as ATP); Terrell, "Address of Judge A. W. Terrell," p. 103; "Two Interesting Wills," p. 1521; Bedichek, "The Patron Saint," pp. 482–83; Vinson, "The University Crosses the Bar," p. 284; Joseph F. Wall, *Andrew Carnegie,* pp. ii, 365–66; Basil Y. Neal, "George W. Brackenridge: Citizen and Philanthropist," M.A. thesis, University of Texas, Austin, 1939, pp. 1–40ff; and Sibley, *George W. Brackenridge,* pp. 10–11.
8. Carnegie Steel was a multimillion-dollar corporation, which distributed its products nationwide. On April 1, 1901, Carnegie sold his interest to J. P. Morgan who founded U.S. Steel. See Bobbie Whitten Morgan, "George W. Brackenridge and His Control of San Antonio's Water Supply, 1869–1905," M.A. thesis, Trinity University, San Antonio, 1961. In-

vitation, Box 3H77, George W. Brackenridge Papers, Center for American History, University of Texas, Austin; *San Antonio Express,* Jan. 14, 1912, p. 12A; *Austin American,* July 19, 1936, p. 2; and Thomas A. Franklin, "George W. Brackenridge," *The Alcalde* 8 (Mar., 1921): 407.

9. Gilbert M. Denman Jr., Brackenridge Foundation trustee, interview by author, Oct. 21, 1997, San Antonio; *San Antonio Express,* Jan. 14, 1912, p. 12A; *Austin American,* July 19, 1936, p. 2; Carnegie, "Wealth," pp. 653–57; Franklin, "George W. Brackenridge," pp. 409–10; Sibley, *George W. Brackenridge,* p. 9; and Neal, "George W. Brackenridge," p. 35.

10. See Dick McCracken, *The Incarnate Word Guest House: Brackenridge Villa, 1852–1969.* Brackenridge to Terrell, June 7, 1911, Box 2H12, ATP; *Tempo,* June 30, 1968, vertical file, George W. Brackenridge, Center for American History, University of Texas, Austin (hereafter cited as BVF); *San Antonio Express,* Jan. 14, 1912, p. 12A; Dec. 29, 1920, p. 6; *Austin American,* July 19, 1936, p. 2; Carnegie, "Wealth," pp. 661–62; Terrell, "Address of Judge A. W. Terrell," p. 103; Sibley, *George W. Brackenridge,* pp. 15, 127, 139–40, 164; and Neal, "George W. Brackenridge," p. 31.

11. Brackenridge to Terrell, Oct. 29, 1894, ATP; *San Antonio Express,* Dec. 26, 1921, p. 8; *Austin American,* July 19, 1936, p. 2; and Carnegie, "Wealth," pp. 658, 661–62.

12. Brackenridge to Terrell, Oct. 29, 1894, ATP; "Peregrinusings," *The Alcalde* 8 (Feb., 1921): 316–17; Carnegie, "Wealth," p. 653; and Sibley, *George W. Brackenridge,* pp. 9–10.

13. *San Antonio Express,* Jan. 14, 1912, p. 12A, Dec. 29, 1920, p. 2; Dec. 30, 1920, p. 1; Judith Huchingson, "G. W. Brackenridge: Philanthropic Paradox," p. 8, BVF; Carnegie, "Wealth," pp. 660–63; and Franklin, "George W. Brackenridge," p. 2.

14. Other muckrakers of the era who attacked the abuses of big business included Ida Tarbell in *The History of the Standard Oil Company,* Frank Norris in *The Octopus,* and Upton Sinclair in *The Jungle.* See Washington Gladden, "Tainted Money," *The Outlook* 52 (Nov. 30, 1895): 886; and Washington Gladden, *Recollections,* p. 404.

15. *San Antonio Express,* Jan. 14, 1912, p. 12A; *Austin American,* July 19, 1936, p. 2; Huchingson, "G. W. Brackenridge," p. 8, BVF; Terrell, "Address of Judge A. W. Terrell," p. 105; Vinson, "The University Crosses the Bar," pp. 283–84; and Sibley, *George W. Brackenridge,* pp. 5, 8, 34, 157.

16. George Brackenridge to John T. Brackenridge, June 15, 1889, and Dec. 6, 1904, John T. Brackenridge Papers, Center for American History, University of Texas, Austin; and U.S. Constitution, amend. 16.

17. *San Antonio Express,* Dec. 29, 1920, pp. 2, 6, and Dec. 30, 1920, pp. 1–2; and Carnegie, "Wealth," p. 664.

18. *San Antonio Express,* Dec. 26, 1921, p. 8; *Austin American,* Jan. 11, 1921, p. 1A; *The Brackenridge Foundation,* pp. 6–7; and Sibley, *George W. Brackenridge,* p. 254.

19. Kathleen D. McCarthy, "The Gospel of Wealth: American Giving in Theory and Practice," *Philanthropic Giving: Studies in Varieties and Goals,* ed. by Richard Magat, pp. 50–51; and Hall, "A Historical Overview of the Private Nonprofit Sector," pp. 9–10.

20. *San Antonio Express,* Dec. 30, 1920, p. 1; Neal, "George W. Brackenridge," p. 36; "George W. Brackenridge," vol. 1, p. 690; and Vinson, "The University Crosses the Bar," pp. 284–94ff.

21. Since 1965 the Texas Legislature removed bequests to tax-exempt foundations from taxation even if they are located outside Texas or the funds used outside the state; Denman interview; *San Antonio Express,* Dec. 26, 1921, p. 8; *Austin American,* Jan. 11, 1921, p. 1A; and *The Brackenridge Foundation,* pp. 1–2.

22. Denman interview; *San Antonio Express,* Dec. 29, 1920, p. 6; *The Brackenridge Foundation,* p. 7; and Sibley, *George W. Brackenridge,* pp. 254–55.

23. Denman interview; *Austin American,* July 19, 1936, p. 2; *The Brackenridge Foundation,* pp. 7, 9, 17; Franklin, "George W. Brackenridge," pp. 407, 410; Neal, "George W. Brackenridge," p. 38; and Sibley, *George W. Brackenridge,* p. 6.

24. Denman interview; *The Brackenridge Foundation,* p. 5; Franklin, "George W. Brackenridge," p. 410; and "George W. Brackenridge," vol. 1, p. 690.

25. *San Antonio Express,* Dec. 29, 1920, p. 6; Dec. 30, 1920, p. 1; David Montejano, *Anglos and Mexicans in the Making of Texas, 1836–1986,* pp. 179–96; and Franklin, "George W. Brackenridge," p. 416.

26. Denman interview; *The Brackenridge Foundation,* p. 9; and Sibley, *George W. Brackenridge,* p. 255.

27. See Lewis and Bowers, eds., *The Foundation Directory,* pp. 465–85ff. See also Donald Fischer, "The Role of Philanthropic Foundations in the Reproduction and Production of Hegemony: Rockefeller Foundation and the Social Sciences," *Sociology* 17 (1983): 206–33. Denman interview; *The Brackenridge Foundation,* pp. 10–17; and John Moore, Brackenridge Foundation trustee, interview by author, Nov. 17, 1997, Trinity University, San Antonio.

28. Denman interview; Moore interview; and *San Antonio Express,* Jan. 14, 1912, p. 12A.

Chapter 2

1. Dealey, also referred to as "the dean of American journalism" and "the first citizen of Texas," died, according to biographer Ernest Sharpe, from a "massive coronary occlusion." Texas press clipping, A6667, File 131, G. B. Dealey Papers, Dallas Historical Society, Dallas (hereafter cited as GBDP); Ernest Sharpe, *G. B. Dealey of the Dallas News,* pp. 239, 275–76, 291, 297; Sam Acheson, "George Bannerman Dealey," *Southwestern Historical Quarterly* 50 (Jan., 1947): 334; Steven L. McDaniel, *Guide to the G. B. Dealey Collection,* pp. ii–iv; and *Dallas Morning News,* Feb. 27, 1946, pp. 1, 10, 12–14.

2. Dealey and his partners held controlling interest in the *Dallas Morning News, Dallas Journal, Semi-Weekly Farm News, Texas Almanac,* and the WFAA radio station. Sharpe, *G. B. Dealey,* pp. 204–29ff; Acheson, "George Bannerman Dealey," pp. 331–34ff; Ted Dealey, *Diaper Days of Dallas,* pp. 121–22; and Joan J. Perez, "George Bannerman Dealey," *New Handbook of Texas,* vol. 2, p. 548.

3. For years the *Galveston Daily News* challenged the *Dallas Morning News* for the designation as "Texas' oldest business institution." See A6667, Files 338, 339, GBDP; "In Memoriam," pp. 3–5, A6667, File 48, GBDP; "A Presentation of the Agreement Creating the Dallas Foundation," p. i, File Dallas Foundation History, Dallas Foundation Archives, Dallas (hereafter cited as DFA); *Dallas Morning News,* Feb. 27, 1946, pp. 1, 12. *The Dallas Foundation 1995 Annual Report,* p. 2; James Howard, *Big D is for Dallas: Chapters in the Twentieth-Century History of Dallas,* p. 107; McDaniel, *The G. B. Dealey Collection,* pp. ii–iv; Sharpe, *G. B. Dealey,* pp. 80–86, 140–46, 151–68, 259–64; and Acheson, "George Bannerman Dealey," pp. 332–34.

4. Winthrop, "A Modell of Christian Charity," p. 68; Tocqueville, *Democracy in America,* vol. 2, p. 485; McCarthy, "The Gospel of Wealth," pp. 46–60ff; and Schlesinger, "The American Way of Life," *St. Louis Post-Dispatch,* Dec. 13, 1953, sec. 2, p. 3.

5. Barr, "The Other Texas," pp. 1–10ff; Wiebe, *The Search for Order, 1877–1920,* p. xiii; and Maxine Holmes and Gerald D. Saxon, eds., *The WPA Dallas Guide and History,* pp. 280–84.

6. Goff, nicknamed "Judge" by his friends, was familiar with the speeches of Sir Arthur Hob-

house who coined the phrase "the dead hand." Charitable bequests, established in perpetuity that later became obsolete, troubled both men. For example, Benjamin Franklin established two loan programs for apprentices in Boston and Philadelphia. By the late nineteenth century such a class was nonexistent. In turn, Bryan Mullanphy, mayor of St. Louis, equally miscalculated when he established a trust in 1851 for travelers passing through the city to the West. Soon thereafter the steady stream of "forty-niners" declined, leaving the fund idle. From gifts to black slaves and orphanages to horse troughs and "wooden legs for Civil War veterans," well-intentioned donors had consistently funded causes that lost their usefulness. Nathaniel R. Howard, *Trust for All Time,* pp. 6–7; Bruce L. Newman, "Pioneers of the Community Foundation Movement," *An Agile Servant: Community Leadership by Community Foundations,* ed. by Richard Magat, pp. 73–88; Horace Coon, *Money To Burn: What the Great American Philanthropic Foundations Do with Their Money,* pp. 1–19; Peter Dobkin Hall, "The Community Foundation in America, 1914–1987," *Philanthropic Giving,* p. 188; Wilmer Shields Rich, *Community Foundations in the United States and Canada, 1914–1961,* pp. 86–91; Ralph Hayes, "Dead Hands and Frozen Funds," *North American Review* 228 (May, 1929): 607–14; Julius Rosenwald, "Principles of Public Giving," *Atlantic Monthly,* May, 1929, pp. 599–602; *Horse Troughs, Bell Ringers, Snuff, Pirate's Captives, Anti Slavery,* pp. 1–6, DFA; and *The Dallas Foundation 1998 Annual Report,* p. 5.

7. Community foundations developed additional advantages and innovations. They created several new types of funds: unrestricted, field of interest, advised, designated, agency endowment, scholarship, and support organizations affiliation. Furthermore, in 1964, the IRS revised its regulations to include community foundations as "public charities," thus allowing higher donor tax deductions. Then, in 1969 the new Tax Reform Act strengthened the guidelines, enlarging the amount from individual donors from 1 to 2 percent, lowering the public support requirement from 33 to 10 percent, and increasing the deductibility of gifts to 50 percent. The IRS also exempted "public charities" from the 4 percent excise tax on investment income as well. Mary Jalonick, Dallas Foundation executive director, interview by author, Oct. 14, 1999, Dallas; *Dallas Community Trust,* pp. 5–6, DFA; *The Dallas Foundation 1998 Annual Report,* p. 7; Hall, "The Community Foundation in America," pp. 183, 187–88, 192–94; and Waldemar Nielsen, *Inside American Philanthropy: The Dramas of Donorship,* pp. 180, 182–87.

8. See Robert B. Fairbanks, *For the City as a Whole: Planning, Politics, and the Public Interest in Dallas, Texas, 1900–1965;* U.S. Bureau of the Census, *Fourteenth Census of the United States, 1920,* vol. 2, p. 133; George B. Tindall, *The Emergence of the New South, 1913–1945,* p. 224; Sharpe, *G. B. Dealey,* pp. 79–279ff; David C. Hammack, "Community Foundation: The Delicate Question of Purpose," *An Agile Servant,* pp. 28–32; and Howard, *Big D,* pp. i, 12–25.

9. Dealey modestly credited Briggs with "starting the movement." Dealey to A. H. Bailey, June 11, 1930, and Dealey to O. D. Montgomery, Apr. 23, 1930, A6667, File 44, GBDP; George Waverley Briggs, "After Thirty Years," pp. 3–15ff, A5864, Box 9, George Waverley Briggs Papers, Dallas Historical Society, Dallas (hereafter cited as GWBP); Briggs to Frank L. McNeny, Apr. 15, 1930, *Archive Book: Dallas Community Trust and Dallas Foundation, 1930–1961,* pp. 1–7, DFA; *The Dallas Foundation 1995 Annual Report,* p. 2; Judith Garrett, *A History of The Dallas Foundation, 1920–1991,* pp. 6–10, 30–31; and Michael V. Hazel, "The Critic Club: Sixty Years of Quiet Leadership," *Legacies* 2 (fall, 1990): 9–17ff.

10. Those in attendance at the Critic Club meeting were E. H. Cary, M. M. Crane, L. M. Dabney, G. B. Dealey, Tom Finty, R. S. Hyer, Charles H. Platter, George W. Briggs, and visitors T. J. Dee and Stewart D. Beckley. Briggs to McNeny, Apr. 15, 1930, *Archive Book,* p. 2, DFA; minutes, Feb. 27, 1922, A5553, Critic Club of Dallas, Dallas Historical Society,

Dallas (hereafter cited as CCP); *Dallas Journal,* Aug. 5, 1929, scrapbook, DFA; and Garrett, *History of The Dallas Foundation,* pp. 2, 6–10.

11. Briggs to McNeny, Apr. 15, 1930, *Archive Book,* p. 3, DFA; and Sharpe, *G. B. Dealey,* pp. 85, 142.

12. The Chamber of Commerce committee members included Chairman Lawrence Miller, J. F. Kimball, J. Q. Dealey, Elmer Scott, and Rhodes S. Baker, who resigned and was replaced by Eugene P. Locke. Article II of the trust agreement stipulated a broad use of funds, including "all institutions, either incorporated or unincorporated, whether now existent or hereafter created, for educational, scientific, medical, surgical, hygienic, musical or artistic purposes, or for the preservation of art, historical records, or relics, or for public beautification, recreation, housing or civic improvement, or for the care of children, or of the aged, the sick, the helpless, the poor, or the incompetent, and all other agencies for the improvement of the moral, mental, social or physical well being of the public." Briggs to McNeny, Apr. 15, 1930, *Archive Book,* pp. 3–5, DFA; C. J. Crampton to Briggs, Mar. 24, 1930, A5864, Box 9, File Chamber of Commerce 1930, GWBP; "A Presentation of the Agreement," pp. 1–2, File Dallas Foundation History, DFA; *Dallas Morning News,* June 30, 1929, scrapbook, DFA; and Garrett, *History of The Dallas Foundation,* pp. 12–20.

13. E. R. Sweney to Dealey, Sept. 6, 1929; Dealey to E. T. Moore, Oct. 4, 1929; Dealey to Eugene P. Locke, Oct. 7, 1929, A6667, File 43, GBDP; Henry P. Edwards to Dealey, Oct. 31, 1929; Robert Lee Bobbitt to Dealey, Nov. 15, 1929, A6667, File 43A, GBDP; Briggs to McNeny, Apr. 15, 1930, *Archive Book,* pp. 6–7, DFA; Dealey to O. D. Montgomery, Apr. 23, 1930, A6667, File 44, GBDP; Dealey to Briggs, Oct. 22, 1930, A6667, File 44A, GBDP; Briggs, "After Thirty Years," p. 7, GWBP; and Sharpe, *G. B. Dealey,* p. 278.

14. The first board of governors served staggered terms: Brown, four years; Flippen, six years; McDonough, one year; McNeny, seven years; Moore, three years; Munger, five years; and Titche, two years. In 2000, The Dallas Foundation Board of Governors had nine members. Briggs to McNeny, Apr. 15, 1930, *Archive Book,* p. 5, DFA; Dealey to members of the board of governors, Feb. 26, 1930, A6667, File 45, GBDP; and Garrett, *History of The Dallas Foundation,* pp. 4, 15–16.

15. Dallas Foundation trustees usually served without pay but did receive reimbursement for "all reasonable and authorized expenditure." When board vacancies occurred, the original trust "proposal" specified that persons holding key posts in the district courts and public agencies, rather than a nominating committee, selected the new replacement. In 2000 this practice had changed to an election by the board. At times the IRS questioned community foundations, challenging their use of advised funds. "A Presentation of the Agreement," pp. 9–12, DFA; "In Memoriam," p. 6, GBDP; Jalonick interview; Garrett, *History of The Dallas Foundation,* pp. 14–15; Hall, "The Community Foundation in America," pp. 180–81; Hammack, "Community Foundation," p. 24; Rich, *Community Foundations,* pp. 22–24; and Nielsen, *Inside American Philanthropy,* pp. 182–83.

16. McDonough was Catholic, and Titche was Jewish. Many Dallas women participated in civic reform through club work. See Elizabeth Y. Enstam, *Women and the Creation of Urban Life: Dallas, Texas, 1843–1920,* and Jacquelyn M. McElhaney, *Pauline Periwinkle and Progressive Reform in Dallas.* U.S. Bureau of the Census, *Fifteenth Census of the United States, 1930,* vol. 2, p. 130; Howard, *Big D,* pp. 19–22; and Garrett, *History of The Dallas Foundation,* p. 5.

17. Unlike the Cleveland Foundation, The Dallas Foundation used multiple trustees. Members of the initial Dallas Clearing House Association included: First National Bank, National Bank of Commerce, Dallas Bank and Trust Company, Dallas National Bank, Mercantile Bank and Trust Company of Texas, Republic National Bank and Trust Company, Liberty State Bank, and Texas Bank and Trust Company. Briggs to McNeny, Apr. 15, 1930, *Archive*

Book, pp. 5–6, DFA; Briggs to Dealey, Apr. 22, 1930, A6667, File 45, GBDP; Jalonick interview; *Dallas Morning News,* June 30, 1929; Garrett, *History of The Dallas Foundation,* p. 21; Kenneth Prewitt, "Foundations as Mirrors of Public Culture," *American Behavioral Scientist* 42.(Mar., 1999): 981–82; Howard, *Trust for All Time,* p. 12; Rich, *Community Foundations,* p. 22; and Nielsen, *Inside American Philanthropy,* p. 183.

18. Dealey to Hayes, Jan. 5, 1931, A6667, File 46, GBDP; Sharpe, *G. B. Dealey,* p. 247; Holmes and Saxon, eds., *WPA Dallas Guide and History,* p. 284; Hall, "The Community Foundation in America," pp. 190–92; George H. Santerre, *Dallas: First Hundred Years, 1856–1956,* pp. 41–42; *The Dallas Foundation 2000 Annual Report,* p. 6; Hammack, "Community Foundation," p. 32; and Rich, *Community Foundations,* p. 12.

19. Briggs, "After Thirty Years," p. 8, GWBP; Dealey to Montgomery, Apr. 23, 1930, GBDP; Dealey to Hayes, Jan. 15, 1931, A6667, File 46, GBDP; Hayes to Dealey, Jan. 23, 1931, A6667, File 46, GBDP; *Dallas Morning News,* Feb. 27, 1946, p. 13; Ben Procter, "Texas from Depression through World War II," *The Texas Heritage,* ed. by Ben Procter and Archie P. McDonald, pp. 165–86ff; and Sharpe, *G. B. Dealey,* pp. 246–58ff, 279.

20. *The Dallas Foundation 2000 Annual Report,* pp. 4–5.

21. *Dallas Morning News,* June 12, 1940, scrapbook, DFA; *The Dallas Foundation 2000 Annual Report,* pp. 6–7; Briggs to McNeny, Apr. 15, 1930, *Archive Book,* p. 7, DFA; and Garrett, *History of The Dallas Foundation,* p. 3.

22. According to newspaper accounts, Dealey died at his residence "only a few hours after his heart suddenly weakened." Locke died "unexpectedly" following a physical checkup at the Dallas Medical and Surgical Clinic. Dealey to Montgomery, Apr. 23, 1930, GBDP; Briggs, "After Thirty Years," pp. 8–9, GWBP; *Dallas Morning News,* Mar. 6–7, 1946, scrapbook, DFA; *Dallas Morning News,* Feb. 27, 1946, p. 1, and June 24, 1979, p. 33A; *To Carry on Their Dream: Dallas Foundation,* p. 1, DFA; "In Memoriam," pp. 1–7ff, GBDP; and *Into Another Year of Service,* p. 3, DFA.

23. Jalonick interview; Garrett, *History of The Dallas Foundation,* pp. 6–10; minutes, Sept. 18, 1939, CCP; Char Miller and David R. Johnson, "The Rise of Urban Texas," *Urban Texas: Politics and Development,* ed. by Char Miller and Heywood T. Saunders, pp. 17–20; Robert B. Fairbanks, "Dallas in the 1940s: The Challenges and Opportunities," *Urban Texas,* pp. 141–53ff; and Hall, "The Community Foundation in America," p. 193.

Chapter 3

1. Jones had $50 billion to disburse but only used $35 billion. For a history of the Reconstruction Finance Corporation, see Jesse H. Jones and Edward Angly, *Fifty Billion Dollars: My Thirteen Years with the RFC, 1932–1945,* and James S. Olson, *Saving Capitalism: The Reconstruction Finance Corporation and the New Deal, 1933–1940.* See also *Houston,* Oct., 1940, p. 2, Box 3M487, File Magazine Files: Misc. articles, 1940, Jesse H. Jones Papers, Center for American History, Austin (hereafter referred to JHJP); clipping, *Houston Business Journal,* Feb. 26, 1979, pp. 26–27, Box 37, File Publicity, 1974–79, Houston Endowment Archives, Houston (hereafter referred to as HEA); clipping, *St. Louis Post-Dispatch,* May 15, 1938, Box 36, File Publicity, 1938, HEA; June 2, 1956, p. 6; *Saturday Evening Post,* Nov. 30, 1940, p. 92; Dec. 7, 1940, p. 29; clipping, *Dallas News,* June 7, 1956, vertical file, File Jesse H. Jones, Center for American History, Austin (hereafter referred to as JVF); clipping, *Houston Post,* Apr. 21, 1934, JVF; Bascom N. Timmons, *Jesse H. Jones: The Man and the Statesman,* pp. 280–82; Jordan A. Schwarz, *The New Dealers: Power Politics in the Age of Roosevelt,* pp. 59–95.

2. *Saturday Evening Post,* Dec. 7, 1940, p. 108; Walter L. Buenger, "Between Community and Corporation: The Southern Roots of Jesse H. Jones and the Reconstruction Finance Corporation," *The Journal of Southern History* 46 (Aug., 1990): 481–510; and Tindall, *The Emergence of the New South, 1913–1945,* pp. 458–59.

3. Russell H. Conwell, *Acres of Diamonds,* pp. 1–54ff; address of Jesse Jones at fifty-first commencement of Temple University, Philadelphia, Pa., June 10, 1937, p. 11, File Jesse H. Jones, Speeches and Letters, JVF; clipping, *Newsweek,* June 5, 1954, Box 3M487, File Magazine Files: Misc. arts., 1954, JHJP; J. A. Elkins to Jesse H. Jones, Jan. 13, 1928, File Quotes, HEA; U.S. Census, *Statistical Abstract of the United States: 1940,* p. 27; *Houston Endowment, Inc. 1997 Annual Report,* p. 13; *Houston Post,* June 2, 1956, pp. 6, 9; Marguerite Johnston, *Houston: The Unknown City, 1836–1946,* pp. 186–87, 274–77; Marilyn McAdams Sibley, *The Port of Houston,* pp. 24–78; and David G. McComb, "Houston, Texas," *New Handbook of Texas,* vol. 3, p. 722.

4. *Saturday Evening Post,* Dec. 7, 1940, p. 107; clipping, *American Mercury,* Box 3M448, File Magazine File, *American Mercury,* JHJP; *Houston Business Journal,* p. 24, HEA; clipping, *Houston Post,* Apr. 21, 1934, JVF; *Houston Post,* June 2, 1956, p. 6; Lionel V. Patenaude, "Jesse Holman Jones," *New Handbook of Texas,* vol. 3, p. 984; and Timmons, *Jesse H. Jones,* pp. 19–20, 49–73ff.

5. Jones retained one sawmill, managed by longtime friend Joe Didiot. See clipping, *The Alice Echo,* Sept. 2, 1943, Box 3M486, File Magazine Files, JHJP; clipping, *Reader's Digest,* Box 3M448, File Magazine Files: *Reader's Digest,* 1929–40, JHJP; clipping, *Reader's Digest,* Box 3M487, File Magazine Files: *Reader's Digest,* 1940, JHJP; clipping, *Newsweek,* JHJP; clipping, *Houston Post,* Apr. 21, 1934, JVF; clipping, *San Antonio Light,* Feb. 2, 1949, JVF; clipping, *Houston Business Journal,* pp. 24–25, HEA; *Saturday Evening Post,* Dec. 7, 1940, p. 107; *Houston Post,* June 2, 1956, pp. 6, 8–9; *Houston Chronicle,* June 2, 1956, pp. 4–5; *1997 Annual Report,* p. 13; *Brother, Can You Spare a Billion? The Story of Jesse H. Jones,* prod. and dir. by Eric Strange, 56 min., Spy Pond Productions, Houston Public Television, 1998, videocassette; Patenaude, "Jesse Holman Jones," p. 985; manuscript by Steven Fenberg in possession of author; and Timmons, *Jesse H. Jones,* pp. 72, 76–77, 117.

6. Jones endowed his foundation with Commerce Company stock valued at over $1.7 million. Due to incomplete data and reportage, the only known larger foundation at the time was the M. D. Anderson Foundation of Houston. See clipping, Box 3M497, File News Clippings: June, 1913–Dec., 1920, JHJP; clipping, *The Alice Echo,* JHJP; clipping, *Houston Business Journal,* pp. 24–25, HEA; clipping, *Houston Post,* Apr. 21, 1934, JVF; *Saturday Evening Post,* Dec. 7, 1940, p. 29; *Houston Post,* June 2, 1956, pp. 6, 9; and *Houston Endowment, Inc., 1998 Annual Report,* p. 1.

7. Memorandum, pp. 1–2, Box 3M484, File Book Files, *Jesse H. Jones: The Man and the Statesman,* JHJP; clipping, *The Alice Echo,* JHJP; *A Man Named Jones,* Box 37, File Pantheon of Philanthropy, Hall of Fame, 1979, HEA; *Saturday Evening Post,* Nov. 30, 1940, p. 92; Dec. 7, 1940, p. 107; *Houston Chronicle,* June 2, 1956, p. 3; and Timmons, *Jesse H. Jones,* pp. 129–30.

8. *Houston Chronicle,* June 2, 1956, p. 3; clipping, *The Alice Echo,* Sept. 2, 1943, JHJP; Lubell, *Saturday Evening Post,* Dec. 7, 1940, p. 107; and Hall, "A Historical Overview of the Private Nonprofit Sector," p. 16.

9. Carnegie, "Wealth," pp. 659–64; Jesse H. Jones will, pp. 2–17, Box 16, File will, 1950, codicil, 1933, HEA; clipping, *Dallas News,* Feb. 28, 1956, JVF; clipping, *Texas Press Messenger,* Apr., 1957, JVF; Buenger, "Between Community and Corporation," p. 491; and Timmons, *Jesse H. Jones,* p. 117.

10. Jesse H. Jones, "Love for Fellow Men Was Proven in Those Days," *Red Cross Courier,* Apr.

1, 1927, pp. 11–13, Box 3M448, File Magazine Files, JHJP; Jesse H. Jones to Woodrow Wilson, Feb. 28, 1919, Box 3M410, File Early Personal Files: American Red Cross, Corres. 1917–19, JHJP; Martha E. Griffiths, "Jesse Holman Jones," p. 2, Box 36, File Publicity, 1939, HEA; pamphlet, p. 3, Box 37, File Publicity 1974–79, HEA; *Saturday Evening Post,* Dec. 7, 1940, pp. 29, 107; Johnston, *Houston,* p. 199; *1997 Annual Report,* p. 14; Buenger, "Between Community and Corporation," pp. 492–94; and Timmons, *Jesse H. Jones,* pp. 101–10.

11. See Herbert H. Hoover, *American Individualism.* See also Jesse H. Jones speech, June 16, 1925, File Quotes, HEA.

12. McCarthy, "The Gospel of Wealth: American Giving in Theory and Practice," pp. 56–57, 60; Procter, "Texas From Depression Through World War II, 1929–1945," pp. 165–86ff; and Buenger, "Between Community and Corporation," pp. 482–85.

13. The number of unpaid trustees varied from three to nine. The Houston Endowment received tax-exempt status on March 3, 1938. See Jesse H. Jones speech to RFC, Jan. 2, 1937, p. 3, Box 3M501, File Speech Files: Interview, Worldwide Broadcast, 1937, JHJP; questionnaire answers, pp. i, 1, Box 3M491, File Misc. Files: Houston Endowment, Inc. Info., Questionnaire 1952–1953, JHJP; Houston Endowment, Inc., contributions to endowment fund, Box Business, File Financial Information, 1937–46, HEA; clipping, *Houston Chronicle,* May 15, 1960, JVF; *Houston Chronicle,* July 27, 1956, pp. 1, 17; Waldemar A. Nielsen, *The Big Foundations,* p. 58; Waldemar A. Nielsen, *The Golden Donors: A New Anatomy of the Great Foundations,* p. 336; and Schwartz, *The New Dealers,* p. 66.

14. Like many other philanthropists, Jesse Jones and the Houston Endowment received thousands of "begging letters" from individuals and organizations asking for money. See letters, Box 3M429, File Personal Files, Appeal Letters, June–Aug., 1954, JHJP; Houston Endowment, Inc., gifts, 1937–46, Box Business, File Financial Information, 1937–46, HEA; clipping, *Dallas News,* Nov. 4, 1945, JVF; and Steven Fenberg, Houston Endowment community affairs coordinator, interview by author, Apr. 25, 2000, Houston.

15. *Houston Endowment, Inc.: A Report of the First Twenty-five Years,* pp. 4–5, Box 3M491, File Misc. Files: Houston Endowment, Inc., Info., Questionnaire, 1952–53, JHJP; questionnaire answers, pp. 1–2, JHJP; Jesse Jones to Mike Hogg and Raymond Dickson, June 13, 1924, File Quotes, HEA; *Houston Post,* June 2, 1956, p. 6; Fenberg interview; *1998 Annual Report,* pp. 76–77; Timmons, *Jesse H. Jones,* pp. 377–78; Olson, *Saving Capitalism,* p. 49.

16. Questionnaire answers, pp. 2, 28, JHJP; Background—Mrs. Jesse Holman Jones, p. 6, Box 3M472, File Posthumous Files, Texas Heritage Foundation release, 5-27-58, JHJP; Timmons, *Jesse H. Jones,* p. 377; and Carnegie, "Wealth," p. 663.

17. Background—Mrs. Jesse Holman Jones, pp. 6–7, JHJP; *Woman's Home Companion,* Aug. 9, 1943, File Quotes, HEA; Teresa Odendahl, *Charity Begins at Home: Generosity and Self-Interest Among the Philanthropic Elite,* pp. 100–18; and Timmons, *Jesse H. Jones,* p. 115.

18. Questionnaire answers, pp. 25–28, JHJP; clipping, *Houston Business Journal,* p. 27, HEA; William N. Blanton to Jesse H. Jones, Nov. 18, 1955, File Quotes, HEA; *1998 Annual Report,* pp. 77–78; and Timmons, *Jesse H. Jones,* pp. 376–77.

19. Jones resigned from public office due to a spectacular feud with Vice President Henry A. Wallace. See Jesse Jones to F. J. Heyne, Nov. 15, 1946, Box Business, File JHJ Government salary, 1946, HEA; Jesse Jones to Herbert B. Swope, Feb. 21, 1946, File Quotes, HEA; *1998 Annual Report,* p. 77; *Houston Chronicle,* June 2, 1956, p. 3; and Joe R. Feagin, *Free Enterprise City: Houston in Political-Economic Perspective,* pp. 7–10, 43–72.

20. Speech, Box 3M501, File Speech Files: Radio Broadcast, Houston, Mar. 20, 1937, pp. 2–3, JHJP; Cary D. Wintz, *Blacks in Houston,* pp. 10–30ff; Feagin, *Free Enterprise City,* pp. 120–21, 240–46; and Johnston, *Houston,* pp. 314–16.

21. See John H. Stanfield, *Philanthropy and Jim Crow in American Social Science.* See also Contributions to Negro Institutions, Nov. 28, 1955, Box Donations, File "Negro" Institutions, 1955, HEA; speech, Jesse Jones to Texas University for Negroes, July 19, 1950, File Quotes, HEA; Feagin, *Free Enterprise City,* pp. 243–44; Timmons, *Jesse H. Jones,* p. 121.

22. Marion R. Fremont-Smith, *Foundations and Government: State and Federal Law and Supervision,* pp. 356–73; Whitaker, *The Philanthropoids,* pp. 17–113ff; and Hall, "A Historical Overview of the Private Nonprofit Sector," pp. 18–20.

23. See Revenue Act of 1950, *Statutes at Large* 64 (1950): 947. George A. Butler to John T. Jones Jr., Apr. 13, 1953, pp. 1–10, Box Business, File George Butler Opinion, 1953, HEA.

24. According to its own report, the Houston Endowment remarkably expended less than 1 percent of its total income on salaries and other administrative costs. After 1959 the foundation began issuing annual reports after twenty-two years of operation. See *A Report of the First Twenty-five Years.* See also House, *Final Report of the Select (Cox) Committee to Investigate Foundations and Other Organizations,* 82d Cong., 2d sess., 1955, H. Rept. 2514 and House, *Report of the Special (Reece) Committee to Investigate Tax-Exempt Foundations,* 83d Cong., 2d sess., 1954, H. Rept. 2681. See also Butler to Jones, pp. 8–10, HEA; and Weaver, *U.S. Philanthropic Foundations,* pp. 172–79.

25. At the time of Jones's death, the assets of the Houston Endowment totaled approximately $31.9 million with an annual income of $7.1 million and grants (1949–55) of $2.7 million. On several occasions in 1955, 1959, 1963, and 1965 the legislature liberalized its grant-making restrictions on bequests to exempt foundations. See Jones will, pp. 1–31ff, HEA; Fenberg interview; *A Report of the First Twenty-five Years,* p. 7; *Houston Chronicle,* June 2, 1956, pp. 1–5; clipping, *Houston Chronicle,* May 15, 1960, JVF; clipping, *Dallas News,* Feb. 28, 1956, JVF; clipping, *Texas Press Messenger,* JVF; and clipping, *Foundation News,* Box 4Y113, File Foundations, RSP.

26. Nielsen, *The Golden Donors,* pp. 335–42; The Jones Empire, Box 37, File Publicity 1969, HEA; and Fenberg manuscript in possession of author.

Chapter 4

1. Throughout her life Ima Hogg endured considerable ridicule concerning her name, which was given by her father. "Ima" was originally the heroine in "The Fate of Marvin," a poem written in 1873 by James Hogg's elder brother Thomas. He apparently never considered the effect of the combined words. See James S. Hogg to John W. Hogg, July 13, 1882, Box 3B111, Ima Hogg Papers, Center for American History, University of Texas, Austin (hereafter cited as IHP); "The Fate of Marvin," *Houston Post,* Sept. 16, 1973, Ima Hogg Scrapbook, Center for American History, University of Texas, Austin (hereafter cited as IHS); *Houston Post,* Mar. 4, 1906, p. 6; Virginia Bernhard, *Ima Hogg: The Governor's Daughter,* pp. 17–19, 50; and Robert C. Cotner, *James Stephen Hogg: A Biography,* pp. 576–77.

2. Cotner ranked Governor Hogg along with Stephen F. Austin, Sam Houston, and John H. Reagan. See James Stephen Hogg Papers, Center for American History, University of Texas, Austin (hereafter cited as JSHP). *Houston Post,* Mar. 4, 1906, pp. 6–8; Cotner, *James Stephen Hogg,* pp. 324–25, 420, 556, 578–86; James P. Hart, "What James Stephen Hogg Means to Texas," *Southwestern Historical Quarterly* 55 (Apr., 1952): 439–47ff; and Robert C. Cotner, "James Stephen Hogg," *New Handbook of Texas,* vol. 3, pp. 652–53.

3. In 1956 the foundation changed its name from the Hogg Foundation for Mental Hygiene to the Hogg Foundation for Mental Health. Gifts, Box 2J322, Will Hogg Papers, Center for American History, University of Texas, Austin (hereafter cited as WHP); will of

Thomas E. Hogg, Box 3R120, file Hogg Foundation, 1944–51, Dudley Kezer Woodward Papers, Center for American History, Austin; financial statements, Box 3B126, IHP; The University of Texas, Hogg Foundation, A Report to the Board of Regents, pp. 1–8; Box 4W241, File: Activities: Statewide, IHP; clipping, *Houston Post,* Aug. 19, 1939, Scrapbook, Box 2J408, WHP; John A. Lomax, *Will Hogg, Texan,* pp. 10–34ff; Arthur Lefevre Jr., "William Clifford Hogg," *New Handbook of Texas,* vol. 3, pp. 654–55; Cotner, *James Stephen Hogg,* p. 584; and Bernhard, *Ima Hogg,* pp. 71–74, 81–84.

4. *Houston Post,* Aug. 21, 1975, pp. 1A, 21A; *Houston Chronicle,* Aug. 21, 1975, sec. 4, p. 4; *For the People of Texas: Fiftieth Anniversary,* p. 1; Lomax, *Will Hogg, Texan,* p. 4; McCarthy, *Noblesse Oblige,* p. ix; Anne Firor Scott, *Making the Invisible Woman Visible,* pp. 149–58ff; and Joan Margaret Fisher, "A Study of Six Women Philanthropists of the Early Twentieth Century," Ph.D. dissertation, The Union Institute, Cincinnati, Ohio, 1992, p. 285.

5. See Barbara Welter, "The Cult of True Womanhood, 1820–1860," *American Quarterly* 18 (summer, 1966): 151–74. James Hogg to Ima Hogg, Nov., 1902, *For the People of Texas,* p. 8; Ima Hogg, "Family Reminiscences," Box 3B130, IHP; *Houston Post,* Aug. 21, 1975, pp. 1A, 21A; Aug. 22, 1975, p. 8B; *Houston Chronicle,* Aug. 21, 1975, sec. 4, p. 4; Bernhard, *Ima Hogg,* pp. 2, 33–92ff; and Louise Kosches Iscoe, *Ima Hogg: First Lady of Texas,* pp. 3–11.

6. Texas women could vote in primary elections in 1918. Texas Constitution (1876), art. VI; A Report to the Board of Regents, p. 1, IHP; and Cary D. Wintz, "Women in Texas," *The Texas Heritage,* pp. 255–87.

7. James Hogg to Ima Hogg, Jan. 26, 1902, Box 2J215, File Sept. 23, 1901–Jan. 26, 1902, JSHP; Will Hogg to Ima Hogg, Dec., 1902, Box 3B130, IHP; James Hogg to Ima Hogg, Apr. 9, 1903, Box 3B111, File family papers: James Stephen Hogg Correspondence, 1882–1904, IHP; Cotner, *James Stephen Hogg,* pp. 568, 583; Lomax, *Will Hogg, Texan,* p. 9; and John Spratt, *The Road to Spindletop: Economic Change in Texas, 1875–1901,* pp. 274–76.

8. James S. Hogg estate records, 1910–11, Box 3B111, File family papers, IHP; Hogg, "Family Reminiscences," p. 2, IHP; and Bernhard, *Ima Hogg,* pp. 65–66.

9. A Report to the Board of Regents, pp. 1–4, IHP; clipping, *Houston Post,* July 16, 1939, Scrapbook, Box 2J408, WHP; Ima Hogg to Dr. Homer Rainey, July 13, 1939, Box 4W239, File Hogg (Ima), 1824–1977, IHP; "Hogg Foundation Inaugurated on Campus," *The Alcalde* 6 (Mar., 1941): 128; *The Hogg Foundation for Mental Health: The First Three Decades, 1940–1970,* p. 13; *For the People of Texas,* p. 3; and Wayne H. Holtzman, "Hogg Foundation for Mental Health," *New Handbook of Texas,* vol. 3, p. 655.

10. The court probated the Hogg will on August 6, 1930. Mike Hogg and twenty-three other plaintiffs filed a lawsuit— *The State of Texas, appellant* v. *Mike Hogg, et al., appellees*—in the Court of Civil Appeals for the First Supreme Judicial District of Texas at Galveston, contesting the demand by the state to recover inheritance and transfer taxes. See Box 3F389, Hogg Family Papers, Center for American History, University of Texas, Austin. See also "will" of Will Hogg, pp. 4–5, Box 2J330, WHP; Hogg to Rainey, July 13, 1939, IHP; Ima Hogg, Condensed Notes, Intent of Trust, p. 1, Box 4W241, File Activities: Statewide, IHP; clipping, *Dallas News,* July 20, 1939, Scrapbook, Box 2J408, WHP; "Final Revised Script For Tomorrow—James Stephen Hogg," pp. 15–16, Box 94-058/13, Bert Kruger Smith Papers, Center for American History, Austin; Ima Hogg to Dr. Harry Ransom, Aug. 31, 1970, *The Hogg Foundation, 1940–1970,* pp. vii–viii; *1994–1995 Annual Report,* p. 6; Iscoe, *Ima Hogg,* p. 27; and Kate S. Kirkland, "For All Houston's Children: Ima Hogg and the Board of Education, 1943–1949," *Southwestern Historical Quarterly* 101 (Apr., 1998): 462.

11. Ima Hogg, interview by Robert L. Sutherland, Nov. 21, 1961, n.p., transcript, p. 2, in possession of author; and clipping, *Houston Post,* July 16, 1939, Scrapbook, WHP.

12. Ima Hogg to Terrill Sledge, July 5, 1946, Box 3B164, IHP; philanthropic, civic, and cultural activities, Box 2.325/D31a, IHP; clipping, *Daily Texan,* Oct. 24, 1963, IHS; and Kirkland, "For All Houston's Children," p. 461.

13. Ima Hogg, "Reminiscences of Life in the Texas Governor's Mansion, 1944–1945," p. 33, Box 4Zg89, IHP; Ima Hogg, "Miss Ima Hogg," TMs, Dec. 6, 1967, p. 3, in possession of author; Ima Hogg interview, p. 2; *For the People of Texas,* pp. 1–4; Judith Sealander, *Private Wealth & Public Life: Foundation Philanthropy and the Reshaping of American Social Policy from the Progressive Era to the New Deal,* pp. 79–99ff; Kate S. Kirkland, "A Wholesome Life: Ima Hogg's Vision for Mental Health Care," *Southwestern Historical Quarterly* 104 (Jan., 2001): 424–25; Iscoe, *Ima Hogg,* p. 7; and Bernhard, *Ima Hogg,* p. 59.

14. Ima Hogg was active in the Community Chest, the Houston Symphony, and numerous historical restoration projects. Ralph E. Culler III, associate director of the Hogg Foundation for Mental Health, interview by author, Aug. 7, 1998, Austin; Ima Hogg interview, p. 3; Hogg, Condensed Notes, p. 2, IHP; Wintz, "Women in Texas," *The Texas Heritage,* pp. 279–81; Anne Firor Scott, *Natural Allies: Women's Associations in American History,* pp. 2–4; Fisher, "A Study of Six Women Philanthropists of the Early Twentieth Century," pp. 322–25ff; and Lori Lee Underwood, "Enlarged Housekeeping: Women and Philanthropy," M. A. thesis, University of Colorado, Boulder, 1997, pp. 30–32.

15. Maud Keeling, former executive director of the Conference of Southwest Foundations, telephone interview by author, Aug. 6, 1998; Odendahl, *Charity Begins at Home,* p. 101; Kathleen D. McCarthy, *Women's Culture: American Philanthropy and Art, 1830–1930,* p. xii; and Kirkland, "For All Houston's Children," pp. 494–95.

16. "Hogg Foundation Reviews Three-Years' Work," *The Alcalde* 5 (Mar., 1944): 123; and *For the People of Texas,* pp. 19–20.

17. Sutherland became director on September 1, 1940. See Robert Lee Sutherland Papers (RSP). Charles Bonjean, Hogg Foundation vice president, interview by Colleen Claybourn, Aug. 17, 1988, Box 3W126, Tape 140, CSFP; Ima Hogg, "Miss Ima Hogg," p. 3; *Houston Post,* Aug. 23, 1975, p. 8B; *The Hogg Foundation, 1940–1970,* pp. 4–7; Kirkland, "A Wholesome Life," p. 443; and Odendahl, *Charity Begins at Home,* p. 115.

18. Ima Hogg interview, pp. 1–6; Ima Hogg, Condensed Notes, pp. 3–5, IHP; Charles M. Bonjean and Bernice Milburn Moore, *Miss Ima: 1882–1982 Centennial Celebration,* pp. 6–17; and Sage, "Opportunities and Responsibilities of Leisured Women," p. 721.

19. Homer P. Rainey to Ima Hogg, June 21, 1940, Box 4W239, File Hogg, Ima, 1824–1977, IHP; The Hogg Foundation inauguration program, Box 4W241, File: Activities: Statewide, IHP; "The Inauguration of the Hogg Foundation," vertical file, Hogg Foundation for Mental Health, Center for American History, University of Texas, Austin; Homer P. Rainey, "A Personal Reminiscence," *The Hogg Foundation, 1940–1970,* pp. 4–5; and "Hogg Foundation Reviews Three-Years' Work," pp. 128, 144.

20. Culler interview; "The Work of the Hogg Foundation," p. 1, Box 4W241, File: Activities: Statewide, IHP; "Hogg Foundation Reviews Three-Years' Work," p. 123; *The Hogg Foundation, 1940–1970,* p. 14; and Holtzman, "Hogg Foundation for Mental Health," vol. 3, p. 655.

21. "Hogg Foundation Reviews Three-Years' Work," p. 123; *The Hogg Foundation, 1940–1970,* pp. 18–19; *For the People of Texas,* pp. 4–5; and *Promoting Responsible and Effective Philanthropy Throughout the Southwest,* p. 1.

22. Kirkland, "A Wholesome Life," p. 445; and *The Hogg Foundation, 1940–1970,* pp. 23–57ff.

23. See *Philanthropy in the Southwest. For the People of Texas,* pp. 7–13ff.

24. Uriel E. Dutton to Ima Hogg, Apr. 5, 1964, pp. 1–2, Box 4W241, File Activities: Statewide, IHP; *Houston Chronicle,* Aug. 21, 1975, sec. 4, p. 4; *Houston Post,* Aug. 22,

1975, p. 8B; Aug. 23, 1975, p. 8A; Ralph E. Culler III and Wayne H. Holtzman, *The Ima Hogg Foundation: Miss Ima's Legacy to the Children of Houston*, pp. 5–31ff; and *For the People of Texas*, p. 16.

25. McIver Furman, chairman of the board of trustees of the Driscoll Foundation, Corpus Christi, Texas, first designated the Hogg Foundation as "the foundations' foundation." Bonjean interview; "Twelve Years of Mental Health Work in Texas," p. 10, Box 2.325/ D21a, File Statewide: Activities, IHP; *The Hogg Foundation, 1940–1970*, pp. 47–57ff; and *1996–1997 Annual Report*, pp. 1–5.

26. Sutherland later died in 1976 at age seventy-three, one year after Ima Hogg. *1969–1970 Annual Report*, p. 51; and *For the People of Texas*, pp. 3–17ff.

27. *Houston Chronicle*, Aug. 21, 1975, sec. 4, p. 4; *Houston Post*, Aug. 22, 1975, p. 8B; Ida Husted Harper, *Life and Work of Susan B. Anthony*, vol. 1, p. 104; and Sage, "Opportunities and Responsibilities of Leisured Women," p. 713.

Chapter 5

1. Although his birth certificate listed him as Giles Amon Carter, he preferred Amon G. Carter. As a civic booster, he was instrumental in numerous projects benefiting Fort Worth including: Phillips Petroleum Company, American Airlines, General Dynamics, General Motors, Meacham Field, Texas-Pacific Union Depot, Will Rogers Memorial Coliseum, St. Joseph's Hospital, and Carswell Air Force Base. *Fort Worth Star-Telegram*, June 24, 1955, pp. 1, 2; June 25, 1955, pp. 2, 8; *Highlights in the Life of Amon G. Carter, 1879–1955*, p. 1, Record Group H, Box 8, File Amon G. Carter, 1955, Amon G. Carter Papers, Texas Christian University, Fort Worth (hereafter cited as AGCP); Amon G. Carter will, p. 29, Record Group H, Box 8, File Amon G. Carter, Personal, 1948, AGCP; Congress, Senate, "Amon G. Carter," 84th Cong., 1st sess., *Congressional Record* 101 (June 28, 1955): 8006–8009; and Samuel E. Kinch Jr., "Amon Carter: Publisher-Salesman," M.A. thesis, University of Texas, Austin, 1965, pp. 64–65.

2. *Fort Worth Star-Telegram*, June 25, 1955, pp. 1–2; Ruth Carter Johnson, memoir for Carter catalogue, Mar., 1965, p. 1, Record Group K, Box 1, File 1972–73, AGCP; "Biography of Amon Carter," Record Group H, Box 8, File Amon G. Carter, 1955, AGCP; Jerry Flemmons, *Amon: The Life of Amon Carter, Sr., of Texas*, pp. 57, 109–22; The Historical Committee of the Fort Worth Petroleum Club, *Oil Legends of Fort Worth*, p. 93; Leonard Sanders, *How Fort Worth Became the Texasmost City, 1849–1920*, pp. 155–56; and Oliver Knight, *Fort Worth: Outpost on the Trinity*, pp. 220–21.

3. See Richard F. Selcer, *Hell's Half Acre: The Life and Legend of a Red-Light District*. U.S. Census, *Statistical Abstract of the United States: 1912*, p. 58; *Fort Worth Star-Telegram*, Oct. 30, 1949, sec. 1, p. 8; Robert H. Talbert, *Cowtown—Metropolis: Case Study of a City's Growth and Structure*, pp. 27–35; Sanders, *Texasmost City*, pp. 40–131ff; and Knight, *Outpost on the Trinity*, pp. 59–166ff.

4. See Frederick Jackson Turner, "The Significance of the Frontier in American History," *Milestones of Thought in the History of Ideas*, ed. by Harold P. Simonson; Ruth Carter Stevenson, Carter Foundation president, interview by author, Mar. 7, 2000, Fort Worth; and Knight, *Outpost on the Trinity*, pp. 123–49ff.

5. *Fort Worth Star-Telegram*, June 24, 1955, p. 1; June 25, 1955; Ben H. Procter, "Amon G. Carter Sr.," *New Handbook of Texas*, vol. 1, p. 998; Seymour V. Connor, *Builders of the Southwest*, pp. 30–33; The Historical Committee, *Oil Legends*, pp. 93–94; Flemmons, *Amon*, pp. 125–56ff; Sanders, *Texasmost City*, p. 156; and Knight, *Outpost on the Trinity*, pp. 221–22.

6. The foremost example of Carter as a picturesque public figure is *Amon* by journalist Jerry Flemmons. See manuscript, pp. 1–4ff, Record Group H, Box 7, File Amon G. Carter, Personal, 1941, AGCP; *Fort Worth Star-Telegram*, June 25, 1955, p. 2; *Fort Worth Star-Telegram, Jr.*, July, 1955, p. 2; and Kinch, "Amon Carter," p. 95.

7. Manuscript, pp. 1–4ff, AGCP; John B. Brewer to the *Fort Worth Star-Telegram*, Dec. 15, 1923, Record Group J, Box 1, AGCP; John Robinson, Carter Foundation executive vice president, interview by author, May 9, 2000, Fort Worth; *Fort Worth Star-Telegram*, June 25, 1955, pp. 2, 8; and *Fort Worth Star-Telegram, Jr.*, Feb. 2, 1954, p. 4; July, 1955, p. 3; Mar. 25, 1978, sec. B, p. 1.

8. Clipping, *The Lake Como Weekly*, Sept. 29, 1955, Scrapbook, Record Group K, Box 2, Katrine Deakins Papers, Texas Christian University, Fort Worth; and Flemmons, *Amon*, p. 15.

9. *Fort Worth Star-Telegram*, Aug. 31, 1947, sec. 3, p. 1; June 24, 1955, p. 2; June 25, 1955, p. 2; and The Historical Committee, *Oil Legends*, p. 94.

10. Radio broadcast transcript, July 14, 1955, p. 3, Record Group H, Box 8, File Amon G. Carter, 1955, AGCP; and *Fort Worth Star-Telegram*, June 25, 1955, p. 2.

11. The first board of directors had staggered terms: Webb Walker served until 1946; James K. Thompson, 1947; Katrine Deakins, 1948; Ruth Carter, 1949; and Amon G. Carter, 1950. Thereafter, directors served for five years after their election. In 1960 the board reduced the number of directors to three and terms to three years. Then, in 1982, after Amon Jr.'s death, the number rose to five again. According to an April 1, 1963, announcement, Carter Foundation overhead from 1947–62 amounted to a meager 2.75 percent of gross operating funds. See Articles of Incorporation and Certificate of Amendment, Amon G. Carter Foundation Archives, Fort Worth (hereafter cited as AGCF); Stevenson interview; Stevenson questionnaire, Apr. 4, 2000, p. 1, in possession of author; *Fort Worth Star-Telegram*, June 25, 1955, p. 2; Lester M. Salamon and Helmut K. Anheier, *Defining the Nonprofit Sector*, p. 295; and Kinch, "Amon Carter," p. 96, n. 5.

12. Nenetta Carter set no geographical restrictions for her funds. Consequently, with her contributions the foundation supported projects such as the restoration of the old capital columns at the National Arboretum and gifts to the National Gallery of Art in Washington, D.C. For discussions on philanthropic motivations, see Nielsen, *Inside American Philanthropy;* Whitaker, *The Philanthropoids;* and Francie Ostrower, *Why the Wealthy Give: The Culture of Elite Philanthropy*. See also Carter will, pp. 16, 29–31, AGCP; Stevenson interview; Stevenson questionnaire, p. 3; *Fort Worth Star-Telegram*, July 2, 1955, pp. 1–2; Nielsen, *The Golden Donors*, p. 335; Flemmons, *Amon*, pp. 298–99; and Kinch, "Amon Carter," pp. 126–27.

13. Stevenson interview; "What Gives in Texas?" *Foundation News*, n.d., pp. 3–4, Box 4Y113, File Foundations, RSP; Hall, "A Historical Overview of the Private Nonprofit Sector," p. 17; and Teresa Odendahl, "Independent Foundations and Wealthy Donors," *Philanthropic Giving*, pp. 167–68.

14. Attorney Sidney Samuels drew up the will following instructions from Amon Carter. See Carter will, pp. 30–31, AGCP; manuscript, Record Group H, Box 13, File Donations and Contributions, 1945–47, AGCP; Carter to Cordell Hull Foundation Executive Secretary Winston S. Dustin, Record Group H, Box 17, File Foundation, 1951–52, AGCP; and Johnson, memoir, AGCP.

15. Articles of Incorporation, p. 1, AGCF; Texas Constitution (1876), art. 1, sec. 26; John Chipman Gray, *The Rule Against Perpetuities*, pp. 670, 710–11; Julius Rosenwald, "The Burden of Wealth," *Saturday Evening Post*, Jan. 5, 1929, p. 13; and Julius Rosenwald, "Principles of Public Giving," *Atlantic Monthly*, May, 1929, pp. 599–606.

16. Carter suffered several heart attacks beginning in 1953. *Fort Worth Star-Telegram*, June 24, 1955, p. 1; June 25, 1955, p. 2; May 10, 1956, p. 8; clipping, *The Pecten*, Sept., 1947, p. 3,

Record Group H, Box 8, File Amon G. Carter Foundation, 1945–47, AGCP; Emerson Andrews to Amon G. Carter, Nov. 17, 1953, Record Group H, Box 8, File Amon G. Carter Foundation, 1953–present, AGCP; Carter will, pp. 14–28ff, AGCP; *Amon G. Carter Foundation 1995 Annual Report*, p. 3; Disposition of Income, Dues, Contributions, etc., 1947–51, pp. 1–12, AGCF; and Kinch, "Amon Carter," pp. 95–97, 102, 124–25.

17. Carter stipulated that the mausoleum was not to exceed $100,000. The final inscription was a collective effort by his family and friends. See Carter will, pp. 5, 14–31ff, AGCP; Stevenson interview, AGCP; and *Fort Worth-Star-Telegram*, July 2, 1955, pp. 1–2; Feb. 28, 1959, pp. 1–2.

18. Carter will, pp. 24–31ff, AGCP; Johnson, memoir, p. 2, AGCP; Stevenson interview; Blaine A. Brownell, *The Urban Ethos in the South, 1920–1930*, pp. 62–63; and Robert F. Durden, *Lasting Legacy to the Carolinas: The Duke Endowment, 1924–1994*, p. x.

19. Carter will, pp. 24–25, AGCP; Johnson, memoir, pp. 1–6ff, AGCP; *Fort Worth Star-Telegram*, Aug. 18, 1963, sec. 4, p. 3; and Flemmons, *Amon*, p. 81.

20. For a discussion of community identity and economic growth see Walter L. Buenger and Joseph A. Pratt, *But Also Good Business: Texas Commerce Banks and the Financing of Houston and Texas, 1886–1986.* Carter will, p. 25, AGCP; clippings, vertical file, Fort Worth Art Museum, clippings, 1904–29, Fort Worth Public Library, Fort Worth (hereafter cited as CVF); *Greater Dallas Area Telephone Directory*, p. 405; *Amon Carter Museum of Western Art*, p. 1; *Fort Worth Builds an Art Center*, pp. 4–12; Brownell, *The Urban Ethos in the South*, pp. 62–63; and Flemmons, *Amon*, p. 309.

21. Ruth Stevenson recalled that her father displayed his art collection at home only in his bedroom until he married third wife Minnie Meacham Smith Carter. The board later expanded the museum focus to include all aspects of American art. See Johnson, memoir, p. 5, AGCP; clipping, Record Group K, Box 1, File 1972–73, AGCP; *Fort Worth Star-Telegram*, Feb. 28, 1959, pp. 1–2; Jan. 25, 1961, p. 3; Aug. 18, 1963, sec. 4, p. 3; Jeff Guinn, "Ruth Carter Johnson," *Ultra*, Sept., 1981, pp. 23–24, Record Group K, Box 2, File 1981, AGCP; George S. Wright, *Monument for a City: Philip Johnson's Design for the Amon Carter Museum*, pp. 5–17ff; Rich Stewart, *A Century of Western Art*, p. 3; *Fort Worth*, Feb., 1961, pp. 11, 46–48; and Bart Pointer, "For the Public Good: Philanthropic Influence in Fort Worth, Texas," M.A. thesis, Texas Christian University, Fort Worth, 2000, pp. 5–18ff.

22. See Revenue Act of 1950, *Statutes at Large* 64 (1950): 947. *Fort Worth Star-Telegram*, May 10, 1957, p. 2; Jan. 29, 1958, pp. 1, 4; July 19, 1958, p. 7; and Kinch, "Amon Carter," pp. 97–98.

23. In 1962 the *Fort Worth Star-Telegram* reported that the Carter Foundation ranked 45th out of 522 organizations under investigation by the Patman committee in terms of operating income. Although a Democrat, Amon G. Carter and the *Fort Worth Star-Telegram* sometimes endorsed Republican candidates such as Dwight D. Eisenhower in 1952. See House, *Chairman's (Patman) Report to the Select Committee on Small Business, Tax-Exempt Foundations and Charitable Trusts: Their Impact on Our Economy*, 87th Cong., 2d sess., 1962. See also Stevenson interview, Stevenson questionnaire, p. 2; and Kinch, "Amon Carter," pp. 98–99.

24. To date, the foundation has issued only two annual reports in 1994 and 1995; Congress, Senate, "Amon G. Carter," *Congressional Record*, pp. 8006–8009ff; Henry David Thoreau, *Walden*, ed. by J. Lyndon Shanley, p. 74; Mark Dowie, *American Foundations: An Investigative History*, p.15; Stevenson interview; Stevenson questionnaire, p. 2; and *Fort Worth Star-Telegram*, July 24, 1962, pp. 1, 6; July 25, 1962, pp. 1, 4; July 28, 1962, p. 1.

25. One by-product of the Patman investigation, which emphasized the necessity for reform,

was the disclosure of the role foundations played as financial conduits for the CIA during the cold war. See House, *Chairman's (Patman) Report.* See also Tax Reform Act of 1969, *Statutes at Large* 83 (1970): 487.

26. The Texas Non-Profit Corporation Act (1959) lifted the ban on perpetuities. Amon Carter Jr. died on July 24, 1982, and Ruth became president. See *Annotated Revised Civil Statutes of the State of Texas* (Vernon's 1997), vol. 3, sec. 1396-1.01 (1959); Stevenson interview; Stevenson questionnaire, p. 3; Robinson interview; Carter will, pp. 14–32, AGCP; Articles of Incorporation, pp. 1–4, AGCF; Certificate of Amendment, pp. 1–4, AGCF; House, *Chairman's (Patman) Report,* pp. 133–34; Bob J. Crow to Phil Shirley, Jan. 14, 1992, vertical file, Amon Carter Foundation, Hogg Foundation Library, Austin; and Flemmons, *Amon,* pp. 294–95.

27. See *Amon G. Carter Foundation 1995 Annual Report.* Stevenson interview; and Stevenson questionnaire, p. 3.

28. See File Foundations, CVF. Jesse Jones to Amon G. Carter, Sept. 17, 1946, Record Group J, Box 7, File Personal 1946, AGCP; Flemmons, *Amon,* pp. 465–67; The Historical Committee, *Oil Legends,* pp. 31–36.

Chapter 6

1. In this paper, the Southwest refers to the states of Texas, Oklahoma, Arizona, New Mexico, and Arkansas. Colorado later joined the CSF. For the number and growth of foundations see Michael N. Tuller and Gina Marie Cantarella, eds., *The Foundation Directory;* Atwood, ed., *The Directory of Texas Foundations;* and Walton and Andrews, eds., *The Foundation Directory.* Conference of Southwest Foundations, *Preliminary Directory,* Box 3.325/V116a, File Preliminary Directory of Texas Foundations and Trust Funds, CSFP; "What is a Foundation?" p. 2, Box 325/V116a, File 1955 Annual Meeting, CSFP; Aris A. Mallas Jr., "Recent Trends Affecting Southwest Foundations," pp. 1–2, Box 2.325/V116a, File 1956, Eighth Annual Conference of Southwest Foundations, CSFP; *Statistical Abstract of the United States, 1950,* p. 14; and James Howard, *Foundation Philanthropy in Texas,* pp. 1–4.

2. The conference began using CSF as its logo in 1955; however, it rarely used the acronym until the 1980s. In 1954 the Conference of Southwest Foundations began compiling a preliminary directory of Texas foundations. Although preceded by earlier, abridged compilations, the first national directory by The Foundation Center in New York did not appear until 1960. "Cooperation," Aug., 1986, p. 1, Box 2.325/V116e, File 1986 Newsletters, CSFP; Maud Keeling, "Proceedings of Conference of Southwest Foundations," Jan. 18, 1957, p. 1, Box 2.325/V116a, File 1957 Conference of Foundations, Los Angeles, CSFP; and Mallas, "Recent Trends Affecting Southwest Foundations," pp. 11–12, CSFP.

3. The H. E. Butt Foundation later relocated to Kerrville, Texas. Lucille DiDomenico, CSF executive director, interview by author, Nov. 1, 1999, Dallas; Margaret C. Scarbrough, "Retrospective," pp. 2–3, Box 2.325/V116d, File 1981 A. C., Margaret Scarbrough's Presentation, CSFP; Maud Keeling, "Remarks to the First Conference of California Foundations," Jan. 18, 1957, p. 1, Box 2.325/V116a, File 1957 Conference of Foundations, Los Angeles, CSFP; Maud Keeling, "Background of the Conference of Southwest Foundations," Feb., 1959, p. 1, Box 2.325/V116a, File 1959 Annual Conference, CSFP; and Keeling, "Proceedings," p. 1, CSFP.

4. The private papers of Mary Holdsworth Butt are currently unavailable to scholars. Scarbrough, "Retrospective," p. 4; Sutherland interview, RSP; Margaret Scarbrough, interview by Colleen Claybourn, Oct. 11, 1985, Colorado Springs, Colo., Box 3W126, Tape A-4,

CSFP; Leonard Holloway, interview by Colleen Claybourn, July 20, 1988, Kerrville, Tex., Box 3W126, Tape 231, CSFP; and Kristy Ozmun, "Mary Elizabeth Holdsworth Butt," *New Handbook of Texas,* p. 869.

5. Along with the founders, the following institutions also sent delegates: M. D. Anderson Foundation, Leo Potishman Foundation, J. W. and Cornelia R. Scarbrough Foundation, Adams Foundation, Carrington Foundation, Hal and Charlie Peterson Foundation, Southwest Research Institute, Foundation of Applied Research, Institute of Inventive Research, Texas A&M University, Texas Society for Mental Health, University of Texas, and the Nix Professional Medical Building. Among the questions arising from the morning discussion were: "How can a foundation board investigate worthy projects?" "What stipulations should be attached to grants?" and "What facts should be known regarding the non-profit tax phase of foundation structure?" "Conference of Representatives of New Foundations and Trust Funds in Texas," Mar. 31, 1949, p. 1, Box 2.325/V116a, File 1949 Meeting, CSFP; "What is a Foundation?" p. 3, CSFP; Keeling, "Remarks," pp. 1–2, CSFP; "Cooperation," Aug., 1986, pp. 1, 8, CSFP; and Andrews, *Philanthropic Foundations,* pp. 340–41.

6. "Conference of Representatives," p. 1, CSFP; minutes of the Foundations' Conference, Apr. 8, 1949, pp. 1–4, Box 2.325/V116a, File 1949 Meeting, CSFP; Scarbrough, "Retrospective," pp. 3–4, CSFP; Keeling, "Proceedings," pp. 1–2, CSFP; Wayne Holtzman, interview by Colleen Claybourn, Oct. 12, 1981, Colorado Springs, Colo., Box 3W127, Tape 161, CSFP; *Conference of Southwest Foundations, 1949–1998, Fiftieth Anniversary,* p. 7; and Maud Keeling, interview by Colleen Claybourn, July 12, 1993, Corpus Christi, Box 3W127, Tape 213, CSFP.

7. Scarbrough, "Retrospective," pp. 3–4, CSFP; Keeling, "Proceedings," pp. 7–8, CSFP; Maud Keeling, interview by Colleen Claybourn, Oct. 2, 1997, San Antonio, Box 3W127, Tape 243, CSFP; Adrian Fowler, interview by Colleen Claybourn, Oct. 2, 1997, San Antonio, Box 3W127, Tape 242, CSFP; Maud Keeling, "A Brief Report of the Sixth Annual Conference of Texas Foundations and Trust Funds," p. 1, Box 2.325/V116a, File 1954 Meeting, CSFP; and Maud Keeling, "Executive Secretary's Report," June, 1954, p. 1, Box 2.325/V116a, File 1954 Meeting, CSFP.

8. Scarbrough, "Retrospective," pp. 3–4, 9, CSFP; Scarbrough interview, CSFP; Keeling interview, Oct. 2, 1997, CSFP; Bert Kruger Smith, interview by Colleen Claybourn, Aug. 17, 1988, Austin, Box 3W126, Tape 140, CSFP; Holtzman interview, CSFP; Sutherland interview, RSP; and "Cooperation," summer, 1981, p. 4, Box 2.325/V116e, File 1981 Newsletters, CSFP.

9. Scarbrough, "Retrospective," pp. 10–11, CSFP; Keeling interview, July 12, 1993, CSFP; Holtzman interview, CSFP; Maud Keeling, minutes, meeting of Board of Directors, Dec. 9, 1957, pp. 2–4, Box 2.325/V116a, File 1957 Board of Directors Meetings, CSFP; "Proposed Plan of Work for the Executive Secretary," Oct., 1957–May, 1958, pp. 1–2, Box 2.325/V116a, File 1957 Board of Directors Meeting, CSFP; "Cooperation," summer, 1981, pp. 1, 3–4, CSFP; and "Cooperation," summer, 1985, p. 3, Box 2.325/V116e, File 1985 Newsletters, CSFP.

10. "Conference with Dr. Andrew Edington and Maud Keeling," July 17, 1964, pp. 1–4, Box 4Y114, File Foundations, RSP; Keeling, "Background," CSFP; Keeling, minutes, pp. 3–4, CSFP; "Conference of Representatives," p. 1, CSFP; DiDomenico interview; Keeling interview, July 12, 1993, CSFP; "Cooperation," summer, 1981, pp. 1, 3, CSFP; and "Cooperation," Aug., 1986, pp. 1, 8, CSFP.

11. Originally known as the Conference of Texas Foundations and Trust Funds, the organization later changed to the Southwest Foundations Conference. This title, however, sounded too much like the Southwest Research Foundation headed by Tom Slick of San Antonio.

As a consequence, the members selected the Conference of Southwest Foundations instead. Keeling interview, Oct. 2, 1997, CSFP; Maud Keeling, "Growing Up in a Hurry!" Apr. 1, 1955, p. 1, Box 2.325/V116a, File 1955 Meeting, CSFP; Keeling, "Background," p. 1, CSFP; 1958 business meeting minutes, "Statement of Aims and Purposes," p. 2, Box 2.325/V116a, File 1958 Annual Conference of S. W. Foundations, CSFP; Keeling, "Proceedings," p. 1, CSFP; "Executive Secretary's Report," p. 1, CSFP; Keeling, minutes, "Report of the Annual Business Meeting," Apr. 20, 1955, p. 7, Box 2.325/V116a, File 1955 Meeting, CSFP; "Announcements, Notes, and News," p. 1, Box 2.325/V116a, File 1955 Meeting, CSFP; *Conference of Southwest Foundations, 1949–1998, Fiftieth Anniversary,* p. 6; and *Business Week,* May 16, 1953, p. 146.

12. Both Tom Slick and Robert Sutherland served the CSF in varying capacities until their deaths. Slick died unexpectedly in a plane crash in 1962; Sutherland retired in 1970 and died in 1976. See Conference of Southwest Foundations, *Preliminary Directory,* CSFP; Keeling, "Remarks," pp. 2–3, CSFP; Keeling, "Growing Up in a Hurry!" pp. 2–3, CSFP; Scarbrough, "Retrospective," p. 3, CSFP; Keeling, "Proceedings," pp. 2–6, CSFP; Keeling, "A Brief Report of the Sixth Annual Conference," pp. 1–3, CSFP; Keeling interview, July 12, 1993, CSFP; and Maud Keeling, "A Brief Report of the Fifth Annual Conference of Texas Foundations and Trust Funds, p. 4, Box 2.325/V116a, File 1953 A. C. of Texas Foundations and Trust Funds, CSFP.

13. Keeling, "Proceedings," pp. 2–3, CSFP; Keeling, "Remarks," pp. 1–2, CSFP; Keeling, "Background," p. 1, CSFP; and program, Fourth Annual Conference of Texas Foundations and Trust Funds, Box 2.325/V116a, File 1952 Conference, CSFP.

14. Scarbrough, "Retrospective," pp. 10–11, CSFP; Keeling, minutes, pp. 3–4, CSFP; 1958 minutes, "Statement of Aims and Purposes," p. 2, CSFP; Andrew Edington, interview by Colleen Claybourn, n.d., San Antonio, Box 3W126, Tape 231, CSFP; Jerry Cartwright, interview by Colleen Claybourn, n.d., n.p., Box 3W126, Tape 151, CSFP; Marshall Wells, interview by Colleen Claybourn, Oct. 1, 1992, San Antonio, Box 3W127, Tape 186, CSFP; Keeling interview, July 12, 1993, CSFP; Lisa McClurkan, "Conference with Edington and Keeling," pp. 1–3, Box 4Y114, File Foundations, RSP; Maud Keeling, telephone interview by author, Sept. 20, 1999; and "Cooperation," Aug., 1986, pp. 1, 8, CSFP.

15. In 1954 the CSF established varying levels of membership: active, $10; contributing, $25; and sustaining, $100; they also raised registration fees to $10 in 1956. The Hogg Foundation continued paying two-thirds of the executive secretary salary. Keeling, "Remarks," pp. 3–4, CSFP; Keeling, "Proceedings," pp. 7–9, CSFP; Keeling, "Executive Secretary's Report," pp. 1–3, CSFP; and Keeling, "A Brief Report of the Sixth Annual Conference," p. 1, CSFP.

16. See also Conference of Southwest Foundations Constitution and bylaws, Box 2.325/V116a, File 1955 First Constitution and bylaws for Conference of Southwest Foundations, CSFP. Keeling, minutes, pp. 3–4, CSFP; 1958 minutes, "Statement of Aims and Purposes," p. 2, CSFP; "Cooperation," Aug., 1986, pp. 1, 8, CSFP; and Keeling interview, July 12, 1992, CSFP.

17. According to Maud Keeling, smaller family foundations historically supported short-term solutions to specific problems. During the last ten years, some foundations have made conscious efforts to secure minority executive staff members who attend the annual meetings. Keeling, minutes, pp. 2–3, CSFP; "Cooperation," summer, 1981, p. 4, CSFP; DiDominico interview; Kathleen S. Kelly, *Effective Fund-Raising Management,* pp. 34–35; Whitaker, *The Philanthropoids,* pp. 14–15; Procter, "Texas from Depression through World War II," pp. 183–85; Wintz, "Women in Texas," pp. 279–84ff; Ann Stromberg, ed., *Philanthropic Foundations in Latin America,* pp. 4–5; Joanne Scanlan, ed., *Cultures of Caring: Philan-*

thropy in Diverse American Communities, pp. 15–18; and Emmett D. Carson, "The Evolution of Black Philanthropy: Patterns of Giving and Voluntarism," *Philanthropic Giving,* pp. 92–102.

18. See House, *Final Report of the Select (Cox) Committee to Investigate Foundations and Other Organizations,* and House, *Report of the Special (Reece) Committee to Investigate Tax-Exempt Foundations.* See also Conference of Southwest Foundations, Box 2.325/V116a, File 1963 Attacks on Foundations, CSFP. Andrews, *Philanthropic Foundations,* pp. 342–47; Howard, *Foundation Philanthropy in Texas,* p. 16; Hall, "A Historical Overview of the Private Non-profit Sector," pp. 18–20; and Bremner, *American Philanthropy,* p. 167.

19. DiDomenico interview; J. George Harrar, "Foundations for the Future," pp. 1–6ff, Box 3M393, File Projects and Conferences, Foundation Executives Group, RSP; and Keeling telephone interview, Sept. 20, 1999.

20. During the cold war several foundations such as the Hobby Foundation served as conduits for CIA funds. See Senate, *Select Committee to Study Governmental Operations with Respect to Intelligence Activities, Final Report,* 94th Cong., 2d sess., 1976. See also House, *Report of the Special (Reece) Committee to Investigate Tax-Exempt Foundations.* Fisher, "The Role of Philanthropic Foundations in the Reproduction and Production of Hegemony," p. 224; Weaver, *U.S. Philanthropic Foundations,* pp. 168–79ff; Prewitt, "Foundations as Mirrors of Public Culture," pp. 977–83ff; and Nielsen, *The Golden Donors,* pp. 4, 24–25.

21. In 1955 the Ford Foundation encouraged serious, independent research into the role of philanthropy in American society. By the mid-1970s the Carnegie and Rockefeller foundations also opened their archives to scholars. Robert L. Sutherland, *To Have and Not Hold: Types of Foundations and of Cooperative Action,* p. 4, Box 2.325/V116a, File 1955 First Constitution and Bylaws for Conference of Southwest Foundations, CSFP; Keeling telephone interview, Sept. 20, 1999; and Sealander, *Private Wealth & Public Life,* pp. 5–6.

22. Gilbert M. Denman Jr., interview by Colleen Claybourn, n.d., n.p., Box 3W126, Tape 151, CSFP; Robert Baker, interview by Colleen Claybourn, June 26, 1987, Galveston, Box 3W126, Tape 7, CSFP; and *Conference of Southwest Foundations, 1949–1998, Fiftieth Anniversary,* pp. 7–8.

23. DiDomenico interview; "Cooperation," Aug., 1986, p. 8, CSFP; *Conference of Southwest Foundations, 1949–1998, Fiftieth Anniversary,* pp. 8–9; and Nielsen, *The Golden Donors,* pp. 334–65.

BIBLIOGRAPHY

Archival Collections and Vertical Files

Amon Carter Foundation. Vertical file. Hogg Foundation Library. Austin.

Brackenridge, George W. Papers. Center for American History. University of Texas. Austin.

Brackenridge, George W. Vertical file. Center for American History. University of Texas. Austin.

Brackenridge, John T. Papers. Center for American History. University of Texas. Austin.

Briggs, George Waverley. Papers. Dallas Historical Society. Dallas.

Carter, Amon G. Papers. Mary Couts Burnett Library. Texas Christian University. Fort Worth.

Carter, Amon G. Foundation Archives. Amon G. Carter Foundation. Fort Worth.

Conference of Southwest Foundation Papers. Center for American History. University of Texas. Austin.

Critic Club of Dallas Papers. Dallas Historical Society. Dallas.

Deakins, Katrine. Papers. Mary Couts Burnett Library. Texas Christian University. Fort Worth.

Dealey, George Bannerman. Papers. Dallas Historical Society. Dallas.

Fort Worth Art Museum. Vertical file. Fort Worth Public Library. Fort Worth.

Hogg Family Papers. Center for American History. University of Texas. Austin.

Hogg Foundation for Mental Health. Vertical file. Center for American History. University of Texas. Austin.

Hogg, Ima. Papers and Scrapbook. Center for American History. University of Texas. Austin.

Hogg, James Stephen. Papers. Center for American History. University of Texas. Austin.

Hogg, Will. Papers and Scrapbook. Center for American History. University of Texas. Austin.

Houston Endowment, Inc. Archives. Houston Endowment, Inc. Houston.

Jones, Jesse Holman. Papers. Center for American History. University of Texas. Austin.

Jones, Jesse Holman. Vertical file. Center for American History. University of Texas. Austin.

Smith, Bert Kruger. Papers. Center for American History. University of Texas. Austin.

Sutherland, Robert Lee. Papers. Center for American History. University of Texas. Austin.

Terrell, Alexander W. Papers. Center for American History. University of Texas. Austin.

The Dallas Foundation Archives. The Dallas Foundation. Dallas.

Woodward, Dudley Kezer. Papers. Center for American History. University of Texas. Austin.

Primary and Secondary Sources

1969–1970 Annual Report. Austin: Hogg Foundation for Mental Health, 1970.

1994–1995 Annual Report. Austin: Hogg Foundation for Mental Health, 1995.

Acheson, Sam. "George Bannerman Dealey." *Southwestern Historical Quarterly* 50 (January, 1947): 331–34.

The American Assembly. *The Future of Foundations.* Englewood Cliffs, N.J.: Prentice-Hall Inc., 1973.

"American Millionaires and their Public Gifts." *Review of Reviews* 7 (February, 1893): 48–60.

Amon G. Carter Foundation 1995 Annual Report. Fort Worth: Amon G. Carter Foundation, 1995.

Amon Carter Museum of Western Art. Fort Worth: Amon Carter Museum, 1973.

Andrews, F. Emerson. *Philanthropic Foundations.* New York: Russell Sage Foundation, 1956.

119

————. *Foundation Watcher.* Lancaster, Pa.: Franklin and Marshall College, 1973.

Annotated Revised Civil Statutes of the State of Texas. Vernon's 1997. 1959.

Archive Book: Dallas Community Trust and Dallas Foundation, 1930–1961. Dallas: n.p., n.d.

Atwood, Frances, ed. *Directory of Texas Foundations.* 19th ed. San Antonio: Nonprofit Resource Center, 2000.

Baker, Robert. Interview by Colleen Claybourn, June 26, 1987, Galveston. Tape recording. Conference of Southwest Foundations Papers. Center for American History. University of Texas. Austin.

Barr, Alwyn. "The Other Texas: Charities and Community in the Lone Star State." *Southwestern Historical Quarterly* 97 (July, 1993): 1–10.

Bedichek, Roy. "The Patron Saint of the University of Texas." *The Alcalde* 5 (April, 1917): 480–86.

Bellamy, Edward. *Looking Backward, 2000–1887.* New York: Penguin Books, 1960.

Bernhard, Virginia. *Ima Hogg: The Governor's Daughter.* Austin: Texas Monthly Press, 1984.

Bonjean, Charles. Interview by Colleen Claybourn, August 17, 1988, Austin. Tape recording. Conference of Southwest Foundations Papers. Center for American History. University of Texas. Austin.

————, and Bernice Milburn Moore. *Miss Ima: 1882–1982 Centennial Celebration.* Austin: Hogg Foundation for Mental Health, n.d.

The Brackenridge Foundation: Fifty Years of Philanthropy, 1920–1950. San Antonio: Brackenridge Foundation, 1970.

Bremner, Robert H. *American Philanthropy.* 2d ed. Chicago: The University of Chicago Press, 1988.

————. *Giving: Charity and Philanthropy in History.* New Brunswick: Transaction Publishers, 1996.

Brother, Can You Spare a Billion? The Story of Jesse H. Jones. Produced and directed by Eric Strange. 56 min. Spy Pond Productions. Houston Public Television, 1998. Videocassette.

Brownwell, Blaine A. *The Urban Ethos in the South, 1920–1930.* Baton Rouge: Louisiana State University Press, 1975.

Bryce, James. *The American Commonwealth.* 2 vols. New York: The Macmillan Company, 1910.

Buenger, Walter L. "Between Community and Corporation: The Southern Roots of Jesse H. Jones and the Reconstruction Finance Corporation." *The Journal of Southern History* 46 (August, 1990): 481–510.

————, and Joseph A. Pratt. *But Also Good Business: Texas Commerce Banks and the Financing of Houston and Texas, 1886–1986.* College Station: Texas A&M University Press, 1986.

Business Week, May 16, 1953.

Carnegie, Andrew. *Autobiography of Andrew Carnegie.* Boston: Houghton Mifflin Company, 1924.

————. "Wealth." *North American Review* 148 (June, 1889): 653–64.

Cartwright, Jerry. Interview by Colleen Claybourn, n.d., n.p. Tape recording. Conference of Southwest Foundations Papers. Center for American History. University of Texas. Austin.

Chambers, M. M. *Charters of Philanthropies: A Study of Selected Trust Instruments, Charters, By-Laws, and Court Decisions.* Boston: The Merrymount Press, 1948.

Clotfelter, Charles T., and Thomas Ehrlich, eds. *Philanthropy and the Nonprofit Sector in a Changing America.* Bloomington: Indiana University Press, 1999.

Conference of Southwest Foundations, 1949–1998, Fiftieth Anniversary. Austin: n.p., 1998.

Congressional Record. 84th Congress, 1st session, 1955.

Conwell, Russell H. *Acres of Diamonds.* Marina del Rey, Calif.: DeVorss & Company, Publishers, 1921.

Coon, Horace. *Money To Burn: What the Great American Philanthropic Foundations Do with their Money.* Freeport, N.Y.: Books for Library Press, 1938.

Cotner, Robert C. *James Stephen Hogg: A Biography.* Austin: University of Texas Press, 1959.

Culler, Ralph E. III. Interview by author, August 7, 1998, Austin. Tape recording. In possession of author.

———, and Wayne H. Holtzman. *The Ima Hogg Foundation: Miss Ima's Legacy to the Children of Houston.* Austin: Hogg Foundation for Mental Health, 1990.

Cuninggim, Merrimon. *Private Money and Public Service: The Role of Foundations in American Society.* New York: McGraw-Hill Book Company, 1972.

Curti, Merle. "American Philanthropy and the National Character." *American Quarterly* 10 (fall, 1958): 420–37.

———. "The History of American Philanthropy as a Field of Research." *American Historical Review* 62 (January, 1957): 352–63.

———. "Tradition and Innovation in America Philanthropy." *Proceedings of the American Philosophical Society* 105 (April, 1961): 146–56.

———; Judith Green; and Roderick Nash. "Anatomy of Giving: Millionaires in the Late 19th Century." *American Quarterly* 15 (1963): 416–35.

Dallas Community Trust. Dallas: Dallas Community Trust, 1929.

The Dallas Foundation 1995 Annual Report. Dallas: The Dallas Foundation, 1995.

The Dallas Foundation 1998 Annual Report. Dallas: The Dallas Foundation, 1998.

The Dallas Foundation 2000 Annual Report. Dallas: The Dallas Foundation, 2000.

Dealey, Ted. *Diaper Days of Dallas.* Dallas: SMU Press, 1966.

Denman, Gilbert M. Jr. Interview by author, October 21, 1997, San Antonio. Tape recording. In possession of author.

———. Interview by Colleen Claybourn, n.d., n.p. Tape recording. Conference of Southwest Foundations Papers. Center for American History. University of Texas. Austin.

DiDomenico, Lucille. Interview by author, November 1, 1999, Dallas. Tape recording. In possession of author.

Disraeli, Benjamin. *Vivian Grey.* 2 vols. London: H. Colburn, 1826.

Dowie, Mark. *American Foundations: An Investigative History.* Cambridge: The MIT Press, 2001.

Durden, Robert F. *Lasting Legacy to the Carolinas: The Duke Endowment, 1924–1994.* Durham: Duke University Press, 1998.

Edington, Andrew. Interview by Colleen Claybourn, n.d., San Antonio. Tape recording. Conference of Southwest Foundations Papers. Center for American History. University of Texas. Austin.

Enstam, Elizabeth Y. *Women and the Creation of Urban Life: Dallas, Texas, 1843–1920.* College Station: Texas A&M University Press, 1998.

Fairbanks, Robert B. *For the City as a Whole: Planning, Politics, and the Public Interest in Dallas, Texas, 1900–1965.* Columbus: Ohio State University Press, 1998.

Feagin, Joe R. *Free Enterprise City: Houston in Political-Economic Perspective.* New Brunswick: Rutgers University Press, 1988.

Fenberg, Steven. Interview by author, April 25, 2000, Houston. Tape recording. In possession of author.

Fisher, Donald. "The Role of Philanthropic Foundations in the Reproduction and Production of Hegemony: Rockefeller Foundation and the Social Sciences." *Sociology* 17 (1983): 206–33.

Fisher, Joan Margaret. "A Study of Six Women Philanthropists of the Early Twentieth Century." Ph.D. dissertation, The Union Institute, Cincinnati, Ohio, 1992.

Flemmons, Jerry. *Amon: The Life of Amon Carter, Sr., of Texas.* Austin: Jenkins Publishing Company, 1978.

For the People of Texas: Fiftieth Anniversary. Austin: Hogg Foundation for Mental Health, 1990.

Fort Worth. February, 1961, pp. 11, 46–48.

Fort Worth Builds an Art Center. Fort Worth: Fort Worth Art Association, 1952.

Fowler, Adrian. Interview by Colleen Claybourn, October 2, 1997, San Antonio. Tape recording. Conference of Southwest Foundations Papers. Center for American History. University of Texas. Austin.

Franklin, Thomas A. "George W. Brackenridge." *The Alcalde* 8 (March, 1921): 406–13.

Fremont-Smith, Marion R. *Foundations and Government: State and Federal Law and Supervision.* New York: Russell Sage Foundation, 1965.

Garrett, Judith. *A History of The Dallas Foundation, 1920–1991.* Dallas: The Dallas Foundation, 1991.

Gates, Frederick T. *Chapters in My Life.* New York: Collier Macmillan Publishers, 1977.

Gladden, Washington. *Recollections.* New York: Houghton Mifflin Company, 1909.

———. "Tainted Money." *The Outlook* 52 (November 30, 1895): 886–87.

Goulden, Joseph C. *The Money Givers.* New York: Random House, 1971.

Gray, John Chipman. *The Rule Against Perpetuities.* Boston: Little, Brown and Company, 1942.

Greater Dallas Area Telephone Directory. Dallas: Southwestern Bell Telephone Co., 1955.

Greene, Jack P., ed. *Settlements to Society, 1584–1763.* New York: McGraw-Hill, 1966.

Hall, Peter Dobkin. *Inventing the Nonprofit Sector, and Other Essays on Philanthropy, Voluntarism, and Nonprofit Organizations.* Baltimore: The Johns Hopkins University Press, 1992.

Harper, Ida Husted. *Life and Work of Susan B. Anthony.* New York: Arno Press, 1969.

Hart, James P. "What James Stephen Hogg Means to Texas." *Southwestern Historical Quarterly* 55 (April, 1952): 439–47.

Hayes, Ralph. "Dead Hands and Frozen Funds." *North American Review* 228 (May, 1929): 607–14.

Hazel, Michael V. "The Critic Club: Sixty Years of Quiet Leadership." *Legacies* 2 (fall, 1990): 9–17.

Heilbroner, Richard L. *The Making of Economic Society.* 9th ed. Englewood Cliffs, N.J.: Prentice-Hall, 1993.

The Historical Committee of the Fort Worth Petroleum Club. *Oil Legends of Fort Worth.* Dallas: Taylor Publishing Company, 1993.

Hobhouse, Sir Arthur. *The Dead Hand: Addresses on the Subject of Endowments and Settlements of Property.* London: Chatto and Windus, 1880.

The Hogg Foundation for Mental Health: The First Three Decades, 1940–1970. Austin: The Hogg Foundation for Mental Health, 1970.

"Hogg Foundation Inaugurated on Campus." *The Alcalde* 6 (March, 1941): 128, 144.

"Hogg Foundation Reviews Three-Years' Work." *The Alcalde* 5 (March, 1944): 123.

Hogg, Ima. Interview by Robert L. Sutherland, November 21, 1961, n.p. Transcript. In possession of author.

————. "Miss Ima Hogg." Typescript. December 6, 1967. In possession of author.

Holmes, Maxine, and Gerald D. Saxon, eds. *The WPA Dallas Guide and History.* Denton: University of North Texas Press, 1992.

Holtzman, Wayne. Interview by Colleen Claybourn, October 12, 1981, Colorado Springs, Colo. Tape recording. Conference of Southwest Foundations Papers. Center for American History. University of Texas. Austin.

Hooper, William T. Jr., ed. *Directory of Texas Foundations.* Austin: n.p., 1975.

————. *Directory of Texas Foundations.* 6th ed. Austin: n.p., 1982.

Hoover, Herbert H. *American Individualism.* Garden City, N.J.: Doubleday, Page and Company, 1922.

Horse Troughs, Bell Ringers, Snuff, Pirate's Captives, Anti Slavery. Dallas: The Dallas Foundation, n.d.

Houston Endowment, Inc. 1997 Annual Report. Houston: Houston Endowment, Inc., 1997.

Houston Endowment, Inc. 1998 Annual Report. Houston: Houston Endowment, Inc., 1998.

Howard, James. *Big D Is for Dallas: Chapters in the Twentieth-Century History of Dallas.* Ann Arbor, Mich.: Edwards Brothers, Inc., 1957.

————. *Foundation Philanthropy in Texas.* Austin: University of Texas Press, 1963.

Howard, Nathaniel R. *Trust for All Time: The Story of the Cleveland Foundation and the Community Trust Movement.* Cleveland: The Cleveland Foundation, 1963.

Howe, Barbara. "The Emergence of the Philanthropic Foundation as an American Social Institution, 1900–1920." Ph.D. dissertation, Cornell University, Ithaca, New York, 1976.

Hyman, Harold M. *Oleander Odyssey: The Kempners of Galveston, Texas, 1854–1980s.* College Station: Texas A&M University Press, 1990.

Into Another Year of Service. Dallas: The Dallas Foundation, n.d.

Iscoe, Louise Kosches. *Ima Hogg: First Lady of Texas.* Austin: The Hogg Foundation for Mental Health, 1976.

Jalonick, Mary. Interview by author, October 14, 1999, Dallas. Tape recording. In possession of author.

Johnston, Marguerite. *Houston: The Unknown City, 1836–1946.* College Station: Texas A&M University Press, 1991.

Jones, Jesse H., and Edward Angly. *Fifty Billion Dollars: My Thirteen Years with the RFC, 1932–1945.* New York: The Macmillan Company, 1951.

Karl, Barry D., and Stanley N. Katz. "Foundations and Ruling Class Elites." *Daedalus* 116 (winter, 1987): 1–40.

Keeling, Maud. Interview by Colleen Claybourn, July 12, 1993, Corpus Christi. Tape recording. Conference of Southwest Foundations Papers. Center for American History. University of Texas. Austin.

————. Interview by Colleen Claybourn, October 2, 1999, San Antonio. Tape recording. Conference of Southwest Foundations Papers. Center for American History. University of Texas. Austin.

————. Telephone interview by author, August 6, 1998, San Antonio. Transcript. In possession of author.

————. Telephone interview by author, September 20, 1999, San Antonio. Transcript. In possession of author.

Kelly, Kathleen S. *Effective Fund-Raising Management.* Mahwah, N.J.: Lawrence Erlbaum Associates, Inc., 1998.

Keppel, Frederick P. *The Foundation: Its Place in American Life.* New York: The Macmillan Company, 1930.

Kinch, Samuel E. Jr. "Amon Carter: Publisher-Salesman." M.A. thesis, University of Texas, Austin, 1965.

Kirkland, Kate S. "For All Houston's Children: Ima Hogg and the Board of Education, 1943–1949." *Southwestern Historical Quarterly* 101 (April, 1988): 461–95.

———. "A Wholesome Life: Ima Hogg's vision for Mental Health Care." *Southwestern Historical Quarterly* 104 (January, 2001): 417–47.

Knight, Oliver. *Fort Worth: Outpost on the Trinity.* Norman: University of Oklahoma Press, 1953. Reprint, Fort Worth: Texas Christian University Press, 1990.

Kuznets, Simon. *Income and Wealth of the United States, Trends and Structures.* 2 vols. Cambridge: Bowers & Bowers, 1952.

Lagemann, Ellen Condliffe, ed. *Philanthropic Foundations: New Scholarship, New Possibilities.* Bloomington: Indiana University Press, 1999.

Lewis, Marianna O., ed. *The Foundation Directory.* 3d ed. New York: Russell Sage Foundation, 1967.

———, and Patricia Bowers, eds. *The Foundation Directory.* 4th ed. New York: Columbia University Press, 1971.

Lindeman, Eduard C. *Wealth and Culture: A Study of One Hundred Foundations and Community Trusts and their Operations during the Decade 1921–1930.* New York: Harcourt, Brace and Company, 1936.

Lomax, John A. *Will Hogg, Texan.* Austin: University of Texas Press, 1956.

Lundberg, Ferdinand. *The Rich and the Super-Rich: A Study in the Power of Money Today.* New York: Lyle Stuart, Inc., 1968.

MacDonald, Dwight. *The Ford Foundation: The Men and the Millions.* New York: Reynal and Company, 1956.

Magat, Richard, ed. *Philanthropic Giving: Studies in Varieties and Goals.* New York: Oxford University Press, 1989.

———. *An Agile Servant: Community Leadership by Community Foundations.* New York: Council on Foundations, 1989.

McCarthy, Kathleen D. *Lady Bountiful Revisited: Women, Philanthropy, and Power.* New Brunswick: Rutgers University Press, 1990.

———. *Noblesse Oblige: Charity & Cultural Philanthropy in Chicago, 1849–1929.* Chicago: The University of Chicago Press, 1982.

———. *Women's Culture: American Philanthropy and Art, 1830–1930.* Chicago: The University of Chicago Press, 1991.

McCracken, Dick. *The Incarnate Word Guest House: Brackenridge Villa, 1852–1969.* San Antonio: First National Bank of San Antonio, 1969.

McDaniel, Steven L. *Guide to the G. B. Dealey Collection.* Dallas: Dallas Historical Society, 1990.

McElhaney, Jacquelyn M. *Pauline Periwinkle and Progressive Reform in Dallas.* College Station: Texas A&M University Press, 1998.

Miller, Char, and Heywood T. Saunders, eds. *Urban Texas: Politics and Development.* College Station: Texas A&M University Press, 1990.

Montejano, David. *Anglos and Mexicans in the Making of Texas, 1836–1986.* Austin: University of Texas Press, 1987.

Moore, John. Telephone interview by author, November 17, 1997, San Antonio. Tape recording. In possession of author.

Morgan, Bobbie Whitten. "George W. Brackenridge and His Control of San Antonio's Water Supply, 1869–1905." M.A. thesis, Trinity University, San Antonio, 1961.

Neal, Basil Y. "George W. Brackenridge: Citizen and Philanthropist." M.A. thesis, University of Texas, Austin, 1939.

Nevins, Allan. *Study in Power: John D. Rockefeller, Industrialist and Philanthropist.* 2 vols. New York: Charles Scribner's Sons, 1953.

Nielsen, Waldemar. *Inside American Philanthropy: The Dramas of Donorship.* Norman: University of Oklahoma Press, 1996.

———. *The Big Foundations.* New York: Columbia University Press, 1972.

———. *The Golden Donors: A New Anatomy of the Great Foundations.* New York: E. P. Dutton, 1985.

Nuffts, Mitchell F., ed. *Foundation Fundamentals.* 5th ed. New York: The Foundation Center, 1994.

Odendahl, Teresa. *Charity Begins At Home: Generosity and Self-Interest Among the Philanthropic Elite.* New York: Basic Books, Inc., Publishers, 1990.

Olson, James S. *Saving Capitalism: The Reconstruction Finance Corporation and the New Deal, 1933–1940.* Princeton: Princeton University Press, 1988.

Ostrower, Francie. *Why the Wealthy Give: The Culture of Elite Philanthropy.* Princeton: Princeton University Press, 1995.

"Peregrinusings." *The Alcalde* 8 (February, 1921): 316–17.

Peyton, Robert L. *Philanthropy: Voluntary Action for the Public Good.* New York: American Council on Education and Macmillan Publishers, 1988.

Philanthropy in the Southwest. Austin: The Hogg Foundation for Mental Health, 1965.

Philanthropy Roundtable. *The Foundation Builders: Brief Biographies of Twelve Great Philanthropists.* Washington, D.C.: The Philanthropy Roundtable, 2000.

Pointer, Bart. "For the Public Good: Philanthropic Influence in Fort Worth, Texas." M.A. thesis, Texas Christian University, Fort Worth, 2000.

Population of the United States in 1860; Compiled from Original Returns of the Eighth Census. Washington, D.C.: Government Printing Office, 1864.

Powell, Walter W., ed. *The Nonprofit Sector: A Research Handbook.* New Haven: Yale University Press, 1987.

Prewitt, Kenneth. "Foundations as Mirrors of Public Culture." *American Behavioral Scientist* 42 (March, 1999): 977–86.

Pritchett, Henry S. "The Use and Abuse of Endowments." *Atlantic Monthly,* October, 1929, pp. 517–24.

Procter, Ben, and Archie P. McDonald, eds. *The Texas Heritage.* 2d ed. Wheeling, Ill.: Harlan Davidson, Inc., 1992.

Promoting Responsible and Effective Philanthropy Throughout the Southwest. Dallas: Conference of Southwest Foundations, n.d.

Putnam, Robert D. *Bowling Alone: The Collapse and Revival of American Community.* New York: Simon & Schuster, 2000.

Reeves, Thomas C., ed. *Foundations Under Fire.* Ithaca: Cornell University, 1970.

Revenue Act of 1950. *Statutes at Large* 64 (1950): 947.

Rich, Wilmer Shields, ed. *American Foundations and Their Fields.* 7th ed. New York: Raymond Rich Associates and Marts and Lundy, Inc., 1955.

————. *Community Foundations in the United States and Canada, 1914–1961.* New York: National Council on Community Foundations, Inc., 1961.

————, and Neva R. Deardorff, eds. *American Foundations and Their Fields.* 6th ed. New York: Raymond Rich Associates, 1946.

Robinson, John. Interview by author, May 9, 2000, Fort Worth. Transcript. In possession of author.

Robinson, Louie, Jr. *The Black Millionaires.* New York: Pyramid Books, 1972.

Rockefeller, John D. *Random Reminiscences of Men and Events.* New York: Arno Press, 1973.

Rosenwald, Julius. "Principles of Public Giving," *Atlantic Monthly,* May, 1929, pp. 599–606.

————. "The Trend Away for Perpetuities." *Atlantic Monthly,* December, 1930, pp. 741–49.

Russell Sage Foundation. *Report of the Princeton Conference on the History of Philanthropy in the United States.* New York: Russell Sage Foundation, 1956.

Sage, Margaret Olivia. "Opportunities and Responsibilities of Leisured Women." *North American Review* 181 (November, 1905): 712–21.

Salamon, Lester M. *America's Nonprofit Sector: A Primer.* 2d ed. New York: The Foundation Center, 1999.

————, and Helmut K. Anheier. *Defining the Nonprofit Sector.* New York: Manchester University Press, 1997.

Sanders, Leonard. *How Fort Worth Became the Texasmost City.* Fort Worth: Texas Christian University Press, 1973.

Santerre, George H. *Dallas: First Hundred Years, 1856–1956.* Dallas: The Book Craft, Inc., 1956.

Saturday Evening Post, January 5, 1929; November 30, 1940; December 7, 1940.

Scanlan, Joanne, ed. *Cultures of Caring: Philanthropy in Diverse American Communities.* New York: Council on Foundations, 1999.

Scarbrough, Margaret. Interview by Colleen Claybourn, October 11, 1985, Colorado Springs, Colo. Tape recording. Conference of Southwest Foundations Papers. Center for American History. University of Texas. Austin.

Schwarz, Jordan A. *The New Dealers: Power Politics in the Age of Roosevelt.* New York: Alfred A. Knopf, 1993.

Scott, Anne Firor. *Making the Invisible Woman Visible.* Chicago: University of Illinois Press, 1984.

————. *Natural Allies: Women's Associations in American History.* Chicago: University of Illinois, 1993.

Sealander, Judith. *Private Wealth & Public Life: Foundation Philanthropy and the Reshaping of American Social Policy from the Progressive Era to the New Deal.* Baltimore: The Johns Hopkins University Press, 1997.

Selcer, Richard F. *Hell's Half Acre: The Life and Legend of a Red-Light District.* Fort Worth: Texas Christian University Press, 1991.

Sharpe, Ernest. *G. B. Dealey of the Dallas News.* New York: Henry Holt and Company, 1955.

Sibley, Marilyn McAdams. *George W. Brackenridge: Maverick Philanthropist.* Austin: University of Texas Press, 1973.

————. *The Port of Houston.* Austin: University of Texas Press, 1968.

Simonson, Harold P., ed. *Milestones of Thought in the History of Ideas.* New York: Frederick Ungar Publishing Company, 1963.

Smith, Bert Kruger. Interview by Colleen Claybourn, August 17, 1988, Austin. Tape recording. Conference of Southwest Foundations Papers. Center for American History. University of Texas. Austin.

Spratt, John. *The Road to Spindletop: Economic Change in Texas, 1875–1901.* Austin: University of Texas Press, 1955.

Stanfield, John H. *Philanthropy and Jim Crow in American Social Science.* Westport, Conn.: Greenwood Press, 1985.

Stevenson, Ruth Carter. Interview by author, March 7, 2000, Fort Worth. Tape recording. In possession of author.

———. Questionnaire. April 4, 2000. In possession of author.

Stewart, Rich. *A Century of Western Art.* Fort Worth: Amon Carter Museum, 1998.

Stromberg, Ann, ed. *Philanthropic Foundations in Latin America.* New York: Russell Sage Foundation, 1968.

Sutherland, Robert L. Interview by Graham Blackstock, October 30, 1971, Austin. Transcript. Robert Sutherland Papers. Center for American History. University of Texas. Austin.

Talbert, Robert H. *Cowtown-Metropolis: Case Study of a City's Growth and Structure.* Fort Worth: Texas Christian University, 1956.

Tax Reform Act of 1969. *Statutes at Large* 83 (1970): 487.

Terrell, A. W. "Address of Judge A. W. Terrell of Austin Presenting the Portrait of Colonel Brackenridge." *The Alcalde* 1 (April, 1913): 103–108.

Thoreau, Henry David. *Walden.* Edited by J. Lyndon Shanley. Princeton: Princeton University Press, 1971.

Til, Jan Van, et al. *Critical Issues in American Philanthropy.* San Francisco: Jossey-Bass Publishers, 1990.

Timmons, Bascom N. *Jesse H. Jones: The Man and the Statesman.* New York: Henry Holt and Company, 1956.

Tindall, George B. *The Emergence of the New South, 1913–1945.* Baton Rouge: Louisiana State University Press, 1967.

To Carry on their Dream: Dallas Foundation. Dallas: Chamber of Commerce, 1961.

Tocqueville, Alexis de. *Democracy in America.* 2 vols. Edited by J. P. Mayer and Max Lerner. New York: Harper & Row, Publishers, 1966.

Tuller, Michael N., and Gina Marie Cantarella, eds. *The Foundation Directory.* New York: The Foundation Center, 1999.

"Two Interesting Wills." *The Alcalde* 10 (November, 1922): 1513–22.

Tyler, Ron, et al., eds. *The New Handbook of Texas.* 6 vols. Austin: The Texas State Historical Association, 1996.

Underwood, Lori Lee. "Enlarged Housekeeping: Women and Philanthropy." M.A. thesis, University of Colorado, Boulder, 1997.

U.S. Bureau of the Census. *Fifteenth Census of the United States, 1930.* Washington, D.C.: Government Printing Office, 1933.

U.S. Bureau of the Census. *Fourteenth Census of the United States, 1920.* Washington, D.C.: Government Printing Office, 1922.

U.S. Census. *Statistical Abstract of the United States.* Washington, D.C.: Government Printing Office, 1912, 1940, 1950, 1960.

U.S. Congress. House. *Chairman's (Patman) Report to the Select Committee on Small Business,*

Tax-Exempt Foundations and Charitable Trusts: Their Impact on the Economy. 87th Congress, 2d session, 1962.

U.S. Congress. House. *Final Report of the Select (Cox) Committee to Investigate Foundations and Other Organizations.* 82d Congress, 2d session, 1955. H.R. 2514.

U.S. Congress. House. *Report of the Special (Reece) Committee to Investigate Tax-Exempt Foundations.* 83d Congress, 2d session, 1954. H.R. 2681.

U.S. Congress. Senate. *Select Committee to Study Governmental Operations with Respect to Intelligence Activities. Final Report.* 94th Congress, 2d session, 1976.

Vinson, Robert E. "The University Crosses the Bar." *Southwestern Historical Quarterly* 40 (January, 1940): 281–94.

Wall, Joseph F. *Andrew Carnegie.* New York: Oxford University Press, 1970.

Walton, Ann D., and F. Emerson Andrews, eds. *The Foundation Directory.* New York: Russell Sage Foundation, 1960.

Walton, Ann D., and Marianna O. Lewis, eds. *The Foundation Directory.* 2d ed. New York: Russell Sage Foundation, 1964.

Weaver, Warren. *U.S. Philanthropic Foundations: Their History, Structure, Management, and Record.* New York: Harper & Row, Publishers, 1967.

Wells, Marshall. Interview by Colleen Claybourn, October 1, 1992, San Antonio. Tape recording. Conference of Southwest Foundations Papers. Center for American History. University of Texas. Austin.

Welter, Barbara. "The Cult of True Womanhood, 1820–1860." *American Quarterly* 18 (summer, 1966): 151–74.

Whitaker, Benjamin C. *The Philanthropoids: Foundations and Society.* New York: William Morrow & Company, 1974.

Wiebe, Robert H. *The Search for Order, 1877–1920.* New York: Hill and Wang, 1967.

Wintz, Cary D. *Blacks in Houston.* Houston: Houston Center for the Humanities, 1982.

Wormser, Rene. *Foundations: Their Power and Influence.* New York: The Devin-Adair Company, 1958.

Wright, George S. *Monument for a City: Philip Johnson's Design for the Amon Carter Museum.* Fort Worth: Amon Carter Museum, 1997.

Wyllie, Irvin G. *The Self-Made Man in America: The Myth of Rags to Riches.* New York: The Free Press, 1966.

INDEX

Page numbers in *italic* type refer to photographs.

ISBN 1-58544-327-1